RASCALS
&
Mickey Rooney
Seabiscuit
Sheikh Bin Had
Fred Hooper
Al Capone
Kelso
Warner Jones
Leslie Combs
Jimmy Jones
Eddie Arcaro

Rascals and Racehorses

A Sporting Man's Life

to Fred and Marjorie
good wishes - - -
Cot Campbell
10-3-02

Rascals and Racehorses

A Sporting Man's Life

W. Cothran Campbell

ECLIPSE PRESS

Lexington, Kentucky

Library of Congress Control Number: 2002101455

ISBN 1-58150-085-8

Printed in the United States
First Edition: September 2002

Distributed to the trade by
National Book Network
4720-A Boston Way, Lanham, MD 20706
1.800.462.6420

a division of The Blood-Horse, Inc.
PUBLISHERS SINCE 1916

Contents

Introduction

***"Four things greater than all things are —
Women and Horses and Power and War."***

— Rudyard Kipling, "Ballad of the King's Jest"

Not noted primarily for being a racing enthusiast, old Rudyard nevertheless understood that the horse ranked right in there with three other supremely powerful motivators when it came to rocking the very soul of mankind.

Like Women and Power and War, Horses — and particularly racehorses — have always had the ability to stretch to precarious tautness the nerve strings of human beings. And horses — like the other three topics — have beckoned to and enslaved a world of supremely colorful, charismatic human beings.

God only knows what the common ingredients are that cause Queen Elizabeth II, the Aga Khan, Sheikh Mohammed, Reba McIntyre, Paul Mellon, Burt Bacharach, Gary Player, on down to Suzie Glutz and Joe Schmo to be engrossed with the capability of a large, four-legged animal to get from Point A to Point B sooner than some other large, four-legged animals.

What could those factors be? I don't really know. But I do believe this: When a person owns a horse, breeds a horse, works around a horse, bets on a horse…or for any reason just pulls for a horse, that beautiful, intriguing animal becomes an extension of one's own persona. And it makes a successful shot to the moon seem possible! It is Hope — always a wonderful commodity.

It is getting ahead of the rest of the world, whether you need to or not. This often foolish quest has always driven mankind: the lottery, the Irish Sweepstakes, unexpected inheritance, hidden treasure...the ultimate, gut-busting, magnificent, thumb-your-nose-at-the-rest-of-the-world score. The racehorse is the ideal conveyance for this deeply intrinsic dream. The racehorse affords you — no matter how glamorous or drab your life may be — the opportunity to strike a mighty blow for the soul.

Edwin Pope, sports editor of the *Miami Herald*, once asked me to explain the essence of owning a racehorse. A tall order!

Trying to be succinct, I said it was like being clad in a tuxedo and walking into a biker's bar teeming with Hell's Angels. But you've got a pit bulldog on a leash!

Several years ago, my wife Anne and I were killing time in our box at Saratoga as a $35,000 claiming race was about to be run. It was a very modest event by Saratoga standards, and since I am an infrequent bettor, definitely of minor interest to me.

Several minutes before the horses loaded in the gate for the mile and one-sixteenth race, three men rushed into the adjacent, empty box. It was not their box; they were just taking advantage of a spot from which to watch a race in which they obviously had particular interest. They were pleasant-looking, middle-aged fellows, dressed casually, and a couple of them were drinking beer. But there was an intensity about them that indicated they were on a mission.

One of them muttered as the horses approached the gate, "Awright, Edgar, now don't screw it up!"

The situation aroused my interest. My detective instincts told me they had a horse in the race, and Edgar Prado must be the jockey. I looked on the program and deduced that the "seven horse" was theirs. She was a six-year-old gray mare, owned by the "Jersey Boys Stable." A quick look at the *Racing Form* told me that Polar Princess was one of those honest, hard-knocking, old campaigners that didn't have a lot of talent but consistently tried like hell. She was 12 to 1 on the tote board.

The boys remained standing in the box (often an easy tip-off to ownership in an upcoming race!) as the horses loaded in front of the stands thirty yards down to our left.

The break came, and as they went through the first turn, the gray Polar Princess was tucked in about eighth in the full field. She was nine lengths from the lead.

The gray-haired man in the windbreaker and floppy golf hat standing nearest us had his glasses trained on the mare, and he murmured, "That's the way, Momma!"

Down the backstretch the horses went in that same order. "Come on, Momma!" I heard him say. Now I'm getting wrapped up in this race!

Into the far turn now, and "Momma" is starting to pick it up a little. She's six lengths out of it, Edgar has her in the clear, and she's got running on her mind!

"Come on, Momma!" A little louder and more insistent this time.

They're at the eighth pole now, and this gray mare is driving! She's three lengths out of it and closing like a freight train.

They're all yelling now. "Come on, Momma!!"

At the sixteenth pole this horse is head and head for the lead, and she's going to get there!

At this point a blood-curdling scream: "Goddamn, Momma! *One time for the boys!*"

One time for the boys. That's what it's all about.

* * *

Horse racing for centuries has provided the ideal stage for reproducing matchless, delicious stories. Perhaps this is so because of the nature of the players. Primarily they are a mix of people who are essentially risk takers (gamblers in one way or another). There are those in quest of a financial "score," there are seekers of social aggrandizement, and always there has been a steady stream of big business high-level achievers looking to add another notch to their belts (Good luck!).

Whatever causes it, it is true that in our ridiculously wonderful sport there exists a plethora of funny, shocking, touching, outrageous, heart-warming, and highly entertaining stories.

Not long ago I wrote a book titled *Lightning in a Jar.* It was a combination autobiography and guide to Thoroughbred ownership. My main problem with writing it, I found, was limiting the number of colorful anecdotes that flowed naturally into the narrative. The ones I did use were quite popular, I believe.

The author has spent much of his rather long life with the horse. And, I am bred to dig the subject. A father, a mother, and a grandfather were people who adored horses and adored the people who pursued them. These antecedents were keen observers of the scene, and they were gifted storytellers. I listened hungrily to them, and then early on I discovered for myself that one of the most charming attractions of the Thoroughbred racing scene was the extraordinary number of delightful characters that inhabit it.

I think it would be fun to tell some of the great yarns of racing's most vivid personalities and equine stars. And, after thirty-five years as an avid player on the stage, I have developed my own anecdotal repertoire.

So here goes *"One time for the boys!"*

1

Stories of a Horse Family

Lexington, Kentucky, in 1937 was a town that didn't amount to much in the big scheme of things. It was really just another semi-country town, but with its own unique charm, in what was in many ways a more gracious and tenderhearted era.

That charm stemmed from the fact that Lexington was then — as it is today — the capital of the horse. In and around Fayette County there dwelled the greatest concentration of high-class horses and horse people in the universe.

Many of the human luminaries congregated at the Phoenix Hotel, the best in town, with the Lafayette, only a short walk down the street, just a tick or two below it. You could walk into the wonderful, old-time lobby of the Phoenix practically any hour of the day and encounter the crème de la crème of the Thoroughbred, Standardbred, and American Saddlebred horse worlds. There the horsemen who would fashion the future of their breeds would be lounging in old, overstuffed leather chairs (with a spittoon beneath every arm). The easily accessed, oak-paneled bar did brisk business throughout the day and much of the night.

In those days hotel lobbies were the nerve centers of their towns. They were the places where you logically met people…for commerce, sociability, or entertainment. In Lexington, the musty, shabbily elegant, spacious Phoenix parlor was the focal point for the creation and dissemination of horse world gossip. Deals were conceived and consummated there.

It was an exciting place. And, somehow it was understood that if you didn't have business in that world, you didn't seek admission. The steady hum of conversation and laughter was often punctuated by the desk clerk's bell or a bellboy's high-pitched page for someone who had received a telephone call or a message (One of the favorite stunts of local wags was to tip the bellboy two bits and tell him to page "Mr. I.P. Freely." The bellboy was on to the joke, of course, but for a quarter he would have done a lot worse than that!)

The cast of characters was invariably clad in rumpled business suits (lots of pot bellies with belt lines hiked up under armpits), wearing hats, and smoking or chewing with gusto.

You would have encountered in that lobby Tom Piatt (breeder of the mighty Alsab), Arthur B. Hancock (father of Bull and grandsire of today's Seth and Arthur), Hal Price Headley (a founder of Keeneland and father of Alice Chandler, Alma Haggin, Pat Green, and Price Headley), John E. Madden (grandfather of Preston Madden), Jock or Sonny Whitney (when they were in town)...and holding forth with an always appreciative — and wary — audience would have been that character of characters, Colonel Phil Chinn.

Some of these gentlemen (and there weren't any ladies reared back in those armchairs in those days) seem to me now to have been pretty old but by no means lacking in vigor. But that may have been because I was only ten years old in 1937, when I made my first visit to Lexington with my father, William T. Campbell.

For several years my father had been a Coca-Cola bottler in Des Moines, Iowa, and had done well enough to put together a fairly high-class stable of three- and five-gaited show horses.

He had bought some of these show horses from horsemen

in Kentucky. And this year he wanted to make a trip to Lexington to expose his son to what was surely the mecca of the horse world. We visited a number of Saddle Horse operations, but both of us also wanted to see some of the legendary Thoroughbreds that were retired or at stud in that area. We went to see Equipoise, Gallant Fox, Omaha, Sir Gallahad, Twenty Grand, and other racing stars.

Seeing those old stars in the flesh was a wonderful experience; but of equal, if not greater, impact was the touching grave marker of the splendid horse Domino. It is a simple marker, and, at the time, surrounded by a stone wall creating a square perhaps eight by eight feet. The stone reads: "Here lies Domino, the fleetest runner the American Turf has ever known, and the gamest and most generous of horses." What eloquence!

Surely a highlight of our Lexington tour was the visit to one of the greatest figures in the history of American sports. This was the fabulous Man o' War.

I would see this swashbuckling red horse twice more before he died, and the memory of these "viewings" has been stamped indelibly in my psyche. I will always believe that Man o' War knew exactly who he was. When you looked at him — and he looked disdainfully back at you — you realized that fact. He just took your breath away, as would the Alps, the Parthenon, or the Taj Mahal!

Nowadays the leading breeding farms in Kentucky have organized tours. Glib guides entertain with a well-structured presentation, as leading stallions are paraded for onlookers. In those days visitors simply drove into the farm, looked around for the stallion groom, and asked him if they could see one or more of the horses in the barn. Inevitably, the groom would be black and definitely mature in years. He would be dressed roughly in some baggy britches with suspenders, a long-sleeved, white shirt and a floppy, bedraggled felt hat (in winter weather add a tattered suit coat).

Man o' War was stabled in a barn on Samuel D. Riddle's Faraway Farm with his own son, American Flag, and one other stallion, I think. The groom, Will Harbut, has become a satellite legend along with the celebrated horse he worshiped. Will spoke in a bass, singsong patois that was made more difficult to understand by the fact the old fellow had pretty well memorized what he would tell you about "Big Red." He loved telling about "Mannawhah," as he called him, but he needed to do his number, get his tip, say goodbye, and get on with his numerous duties in the stud barn.

His signature line, delivered as he stood at the end of the shank gazing up at the big horse, was, "Dis is the mostest hoss that ever was." Indeed he may have been.

At any rate, Man o' War got my attention and planted the seed that a great racehorse, or a great horse of any kind, was a really awesome thing. I was already enamored of the equine species, but it was "Big Red" who caused me to fall hook, line, and sinker for the Thoroughbred racehorse.

Early during that romance, however, I found that any sort of competitive horse activity is inevitably going to create both dark valleys and high peaks. I traveled through one of the darkest of those dark valleys during my show horse career.

My father, when he began to detect the first inkling of success in the soft-drink business, was frantic to own some three- and five-gaited Saddlebreds, a breed that had enchanted him as a youngster. Typical of my father, he flung himself and his family into this hobby with great fervor, and soon Shoestring Stable was a good-sized outfit. We had a professional trainer who schooled the horses and struggled to make me a proficient show rider.

I was a rather rotund little fellow, and my weight caused me enormous trouble getting on a horse. Once I did get astride, with the help of two huffing and puffing grown men, I got to where I could ride a horse pretty well, ultimately becoming champion amateur rider in Iowa, Nebraska, and Missouri.

For actual show ring competition, I was outfitted exceedingly well with two expensive riding outfits: one was butternut brown; the other, dove gray. These ensembles were traditionally very tight and form fitting, and with my form, they caused me to look like an alarmingly plump link sausage.

It was absolutely essential that show horse riders wear this type of tight, restrictive garb, both then and now. That my avoirdupois did not lend itself at all well to this type of clinging habit was just tough luck. No way around it. To wear anything else (a nice, loose-flowing Hawaiian shirt, for instance) would certainly have been more forgiving esthetically, but in the show horse world this drastic departure from sleekness would have been considered unthinkably provincial.

Any self-consciousness in connection with my obesity — and there was considerable — was put to the test one night in Lincoln, Nebraska.

I was showing a horse at the Nebraska State Fair. I was outfitted in my brown jodhpur suit, complete, of course, with a derby hat of the same color. I had perhaps added five or six pounds to my already hard-to-define frame since being fitted for this suit, and every nook and cranny was easily discernible through the tautly stretched fabric.

This was a night event and the arena was packed. The crowd included about seventy-five boys from the famous Father Flanagan's Boys' Town, an orphanage for wayward and homeless boys.

This group was positioned in a bloc, in the cheap seats at the end of the ring, and they were a lively, excited bunch, entirely ready to be entertained by practically anything. It would not take much to set them alight.

When young Campbell and his fancy three-gaited horse

popped into the ring and went energetically posting past this group, believe me, it got their attention! The idea of seeing this fat child (about their own age) clad in such raiment in the first place and vastly overweight — and flaunting it — in the second place was more than their decorum could stand.

Such catcalls, whooping, whistling, and imitative gesticulations you cannot imagine. That I was riding and showing the horse quite well was completely beyond their appreciation. I was simply a very tubby kid, all duded up in such a manner as to accentuate my fatness (and richness), and fair game for their derision.

Unfortunately, their manner of recognition for my efforts was contagious, and soon the entire assemblage in the Lincoln Show Arena was in complete noisy harmony with the lads from Boys' Town.

It made for a miserable thirty minutes. I think I was "tied" second or third. Technically I may have deserved to win, but no judge would have been brave enough to give me the blue ribbon. Not with that crowd on that night. We were all probably better off with those results.

This memorable event can probably be thanked for my present-day obsession with weight control.

You Can Bet On Them?

My first real introduction to the intriguing side of racing horses, and backing them financially, came in New Orleans in the offices of my grandfather, Dick Cothran, a cotton speculator, boulevardier, bon vivant…and a gambling man, if God ever made one.

Dick Cothran was essentially a cotton trader. He lived in New Orleans because it was the site of the New Orleans Cotton Exchange — the place to be if you were serious about trading in the commodity of cotton.

Dick Cothran was known in that environment as a "lightning calculator," which, translated, means he was a fearless gambler and was mighty quick about the mathematics that governed decisions on the trading of cotton.

A distinguished-looking man with a goatee, he was given to wearing wrinkled seersucker and white linen suits and sailor straw hats (which he absent-mindedly kept on his head much of the day and night, often even when clad in a long white nightshirt!). He was a gentleman of a very kindly and jovial nature.

He also adored betting on the horses and was a founding member of the New Orleans Jockey Club.

For years, when he was rolling high in the cotton market, he maintained in his suite of offices a special room in which he had ensconced a professional horse racing handicapper, with telegraph and telephone hook-ups to every major racetrack in North America.

And he bet the horses — through bookmakers — every day of his business life. It was not exactly legal, but who worried about it? It was part of his existence. It was simply his custom! I remember so well as a child the absolute enchantment of visiting this wonderful room, tended to by the lugubrious Edmund, the pale, nervous, chain-smoking handicapper. My grandfather would leave the floor of the exchange periodically during the day and scurry up to the "race room," where he and Edmund would confer over a page from the popular racing paper of that day, *The Morning Telegraph.* There would be some brief, serious murmuring, and then Edmund would nod his head with whatever degree of approval my grandfather's final decision had evinced. He would then call in the bet, usually just a few minutes before post time.

Often, when we came downtown to pick up my grandfather in late afternoon, I was permitted to go in and visit the "race room." Maybe, if the timing was right, I would get to listen through the headphones to a race call of, say, the eighth at

Belmont Park or the third at Tanforan. I can recall even today the excitement, mystery, and the tension of that room.

It had exquisite allure and charisma compared to today's off-track betting parlors, simulcast centers, or the race books in Las Vegas or Atlantic City.

There was no television then. There were no betting windows, no plethora of races running within minutes of each other, no cocktail waitresses in scanty garb, no glitz. There were just old Edmund; the magical earphones; the clacking ticker tape; old-time, stand-up telephone instruments; the alert demeanor of these gambling men; and their quiet, terse phone conversations.

The idea that this exercise revolved around gorgeous horses trying to out-race each other in glamorous, far-off places set me on fire.

And I think often of the delicious thrill of that wonderful May day in 1934 when I put the big earphones on and heard the electrifying call of Cavalcade's Kentucky Derby victory, made so much sweeter by Papa's (my name for my grandfather) having given me two dollars to wager on this special occasion.

Alas, Dick Cothran was wiped out in 1935 — not by the horses, but by the nosedive taken by the cotton market.

Readers with a gambling bent will be delighted that he partially solved his downturn by — of all things — buying a book on how to play poker! Though he had never played poker, he read and completely absorbed this book, memorized the percentages, and in no time could tell you the exact mathematical likelihood of drawing to an inside straight or turning two pair into a full house.

On top of that, he was, after all, a "lightning calculator." If he just knew the rules, why wouldn't he be a superb poker player? Thanks to the book he became one.

In the middle of the 1930s, he supported his family by playing poker three times a week at the better social clubs of New Orleans. When cotton made a comeback, he resumed trading. But thank God for poker in the meantime! He did much better with the poker than he did with the horses, but he never quit trying because he did love a racehorse and a horse race.

Uncle Al

Another factor contributing to my fascination with the racehorse came through a glamorous but ne'er-do-well uncle from Virginia. He had been an inveterate foxhunter, followed racing devoutly, and had ridden with some distinction in steeplechase races.

During the Depression, Uncle Al lived in Atlanta with his wife, my father's sister, known as "Baby," or to me as "Aunt Baby."

Albert Dabney Irving was a native of Charlottesville, Virginia. His family was rather prominent there. And he was a professional Virginian. You'd have thought that Robert E. Lee was a foul-mouthed, degenerate carpetbagger compared to Al. Al had gone to "The University" (of Virginia, of course). He had served his country in France in World War I, and before and after, in civilian life, he had spent much of his time riding races, riding to the hounds, fornicating (voraciously, but with relative style and discretion), drinking, being a gentleman, and avoiding any form of work.

Al was a handsome fellow, with the sleek head of Rudolph Valentino, but with the kind, crinkly eyes of Edmund Gwenn (Santa Claus in *Miracle on 34th Street*). He had "rich boy hair." He parted it about an inch off center, and it was then swept back on either side, having been so arranged by a wide-toothed comb. Liberal usage of Kreml Hair Tonic gave it a sort of permanent, shiny, and etched-in-stone look. He looked like a "gentleman rider" is supposed to look!

Al Irving could charm the birds right out of the trees. He loved horses, and the life that eddied around horses. He really knew something about a horse, particularly a racehorse, and he could wax bewitchingly about its attributes. Stories from him about horses and horse people absolutely enthralled me and further contributed to my falling in love with the idea of men and women racing horses against each other.

Inexplicably — considering his priorities and his aversion to physical labor, unless he was mounted (one way or another!) — he married neither a beautiful nor a wealthy woman. His desired lifestyle would have made it expedient to have done so.

He made his name synonymous with conviviality and joie de vivre one unforgettable evening at the staid old Piedmont Driving Club in Atlanta.

His brother-in-law, George Campbell, was a member, and on a warm, spring night shortly after the end of the war, Al and "Baby" were socializing with a sizeable coterie of friends — some of Atlanta's "beautiful people." Considerable merriment and frolic enlivened this al fresco affair on the lawn at the club, and Al, as usual, had imbibed quite heavily and was feeling no pain. During a lull in the revelry at his table, Al decided that it behooved him to liven up the proceedings.

Quietly slipping into the nearby men's locker room, he went to George's locker, borrowed his bathing suit, disrobed, and excitedly slipped it on.

Then, gleefully, he flung the door open, hurtled out onto the lawn and sprinted madly for the nearby pool, shrieking, "The last one in is a rotten egg!"

With all the spirit of an Australian lifeguard entering the surf, he dove enthusiastically into the pool.

There was no water in the pool.

That broke up the party. And it sure as hell broke up Al. He spent the night in a nearby hospital suffering from a fractured collarbone and a severe hangover! He had certainly had similar physical setbacks during his riding days.

The Influence of Black Gold

My mother, Lila, the daughter of Dick Cothran, also adored the horses.

She married a man who adored them, and they produced a child who certainly did. She was present at one of the most heart-rending, dramatic events in the history of racing — or any sport. Her telling and retelling of it certainly stoked the fires that were lit within me early in my life.

It had to do with a feisty, dark-chocolate brown horse named Black Gold, who possessed the heart of a Cape Town lion. His background would have nourished a grossly exaggerated plot if it were made into a movie. Incidentally, there was a movie.

Black Gold was owned by an Osage Indian woman named Rosa Hoots.

But the saga began with a wonderful little sprinting mare named Useeit, owned by Rosa's husband, Al. Mr. Hoots would have certainly earned immortality on the American Turf without the help of Black Gold. He had already accomplished that — in a dark manner — with Useeit, when he committed *the* unpardonable sin. He ran Useeit in a claiming race and she was claimed, but Hoots refused to release her to the claimant and backed up his bravado with a thirty-eight-caliber revolver! He was, of course, ruled off the Turf.

One of the greatest figures in all of racing — then or now — was touched by Hoots' misguided devotion to the little mare. This was Colonel E.R. Bradley — the legendary gambler-horseman-gentleman. He learned that Hoots, on his deathbed, had a vision that his mare would be bred to the Colonel's very stylish Black Toney and that the issue would win the Kentucky Derby. Bradley sportingly offered a season to Hoots' widow.

The mating produced Black Gold. And he *would* win the Kentucky Derby!

Black Gold was a grand-looking little fellow, and he was a running fool! He came along in the mid-twenties, just after Man o' War, at a time when the sporting public was hungering for heroes.

The colt with the humble background came out smoking as a two-year-old and then blossomed into the very best as a sophomore.

He won the Derby as the favorite in 1924. Half of the Osage Indian Nation had backed him in the winter book at 100-1!

He had a wonderful racing career and much of his campaign centered at the Fair Grounds in New Orleans — at that time one of the finest racetracks in America.

As a four-year-old, the colt was retired to stud, but he proved to be infertile. When the horse was six, Rosa Hoots decided he should try for a comeback. It was to be a sad and unsuccessful campaign, and the entire racing world focused intently on it.

After a few tighteners, Black Gold seemed to be rounding back into form when he ran what was to be the last race of his life. It was a mile race at the Fair Grounds.

The stands were packed to the rafters, and the press from all over the region were on hand to see this crucial comeback race. As usual, Black Gold stalked the pace, and when they entered that long, lonesome Fair Grounds stretch, he put his belly on the ground and made his move. The crowd went berserk. But at the eighth pole, just as he roared into strong contention, his jockey heard a snap. Black Gold's foreleg had given way. The horse stayed on his feet and fought courageously to the finish line, despite the rider's efforts to pull him up.

With the huge crowd now in stunned silence, Black Gold was walked agonizingly, on his own steam, to the paddock under the grandstand where he was put down.

It shook the entire world of racing, and it ravaged his fans in New Orleans and throughout the Southwest where the little fellow was a special hero.

My mother and her father were two of the people on hand for this momentous race.

Immediately after the tragic accident, it was decided that Black Gold should be buried in the infield at the Fair Grounds, next to another equine hero, the great mare Pan Zareta. The funeral was set for two days following the ill-fated race. The papers and the radio were full of news of the horse's death, and the upcoming funeral was well publicized.

New Orleans is a strange town, unlike any other in this country. It has its own ideas of how life should be lived and what is important in this world. For that reason, it is probably not surprising that the parish of Orleans decreed that the public schools would be closed on the day of Black Gold's funeral so that the children of the city, many of whom had long since been caught up in the stagecraft of this wonderful horse's career, could pay tribute at the final curtain.

On a mild January day in 1928, my mother joined the thousands who flocked to the infield of the racetrack to say goodbye to the beloved racehorse.

Many in the crowd were school children. Though schools were officially closed, a number of teachers had volunteered to organize trips in cars or streetcars for those children whose parents were not already taking them.

My mother related that the huge crowd assembled in a circle around the gravesite in the infield. A rather rag-tag jazz band played both mournful and lively numbers, including the great anthem of the Derby, "My Old Kentucky Home." Those who were not already weeping dissolved with that selection. And then "Auld Lang Syne" delivered the finishing touches.

A rather portly man in a dark suit and a derby hat then told

— in a stentorian voice that did not really require the megaphone he employed — of the virtues and accomplishments of Black Gold. A large wooden box, shrouded in black crepe and containing his hooves and heart (this has long been the custom for interments of famous horses), was lowered into the grave and then covered up. The flag was lowered to half-mast and the signal was given for the children to come forward and place their flowers on the grave.

Black Gold was buried. Everyone left the Fair Grounds.

I was born in New Orleans and have always been moderately content with that origin. But the manner in which New Orleans paid tribute to Black Gold makes me exceedingly proud to call the city my birthplace.

2

Life in a Horse Town

If the average horseman were asked to name the great racehorse towns of the world, he would lead with Lexington, Kentucky. Then would probably come Ocala, Florida; Aiken and Camden, South Carolina; Middleburg, Virginia; Saratoga Springs, New York; Chantilly, France; and Newmarket and Lambourn, England. Since I'm the one doing the "supposing," I would add Franklin, Tennessee. It was, and is, plenty horsey, and I have a warm spot in my heart for the town where I did some growing up.

Lexington is the undisputed daddy of all horse towns. But, lamentably, it has become more of a horse "city" in this day. The city and its importance in the horse world have increased steadily in significance, but growth has diminished it slightly in charm, this crotchety observer opines.

The previous chapter, to some extent, touched on Lexington, where, inevitably, many stories told throughout the balance of this work are set.

Aiken

Aiken, South Carolina, is where I live. It is a fine horse town. Much to the disgust of the Aiken progressives, many of the roads there are still dirt to accommodate the safety of racehorses, polo ponies, hunters, and carriage horses.

There are horses of all types all over the place. It is not uncommon in Aiken to see a six-horse hitch, with top-hatted driver and festive passengers, gaily clopping through the main downtown thoroughfare.

Aiken reeks of tradition and of the Thoroughbred establishment. Names like Whitney, Bostwick, Von Stade, Grace, Iselin, Knox, Post, Mellon, and Hitchcock — prominent in *The Social Register*, The Jockey Club, and other blue-blooded rosters — still have distinct ties to this community.

But Aiken does not have the panache it once had in the era when the gentlemen of the "Winter Colony" were whisked out of New York on private, non-stop trains every Friday night and returned to the city on Monday. And so were the young sons and daughters of socialites transported to this South Carolina city near the Georgia line for proper schooling with suitable peers at Aiken Prep or Fermata. Those same trains carried horses, in surprising numbers, to and from Aiken from fall to spring.

The illustrious Greentree Stable was for many years a mainstay on the Aiken equine scene, and it flourished under the iron hand of the exalted, Princeton-educated trainer, John Gaver. His son, Jim, still a resident of Aiken, recently wrote this rather charming remembrance of winter quarters in this racehorse town:

> "As a little boy in Aiken in the late 1940s, I vividly remember the spectacle of the arrival and departure of the Greentree horses. In the fall, a few weeks before Thanksgiving, a special private train from New York would pull alongside the railway freight station on Park Avenue. In those days, each Thoroughbred was attended by its own groom, so the unloading of the train produced a parade of forty or more horses, each perfectly turned out and draped in identical green and white plaid blankets. The horses were led from Park Avenue

down Williamsburg to South Boundary, then along Marlboro Street to the Greentree complex on Two Notch Road. Their grooms would be returning to Aiken after almost eight months; the town was in a holiday mood, welcoming back its men to their families, often a father hugging a new son or daughter for the first time. There were many smiles and much excitement: Greentree was back in town!

"Sadly, the process had to reverse itself in the spring. Still the same magnificent Thoroughbreds in their traveling gear, but now smiles turned to tears as fathers, sons, husbands and boy friends headed north for the summer racing season."

John Gaver would have been the perfect poster boy for Aiken. However, he would have retched at the idea of being a poster boy for anything. He loathed any form of public recognition and despised his inevitable press moniker, "Princeton Johnny." But he did love Aiken and was its uncrowned king.

Gaver trained such stars as Tom Fool, Shut Out, Devil Diver, Capot, Stage Door Johnny, and No Robbery for Greentree and held that prestigious job for almost four decades. In his early career he taught languages at Groton and was a bond salesman, but, through college chums, he was able to connect with Greentree as a stable agent and follow his first love for the rest of his life. He was a marvelous horseman. However, with his tweed jackets, Brooks Brothers button-down shirts, and regimental striped ties, he was not one you would immediately identify as a horse trainer!

His improbable secondary passion in life was the growing of camellias. John Gaver indulged his love for both horses and camellias with great ardor while in Aiken winter quarters.

John was a wonderful, kind man, but he did not suffer fools gladly. Nor could he be described as "approachable."

With a rather stern visage, laconic inclinations, and a gruff way about him, he was not a man you would single out for horseplay. You would take no liberties with John Gaver. He was highly respected and universally revered — one of the great figures of the American Turf.

The old boy was president of the Aiken Training Track for many, many years, and no blade of grass was disturbed without his complete approval.

A younger trainer with whom he shared mutual admiration was MacKenzie Miller, who was to become a figure of equal stature in our industry. Mack learned from Gaver, was greatly influenced by him, and stood in awe of him. And he was anxious not to displease him.

One winter when both men were at the top of their games, Mack was training for Charles Engelhard and had the outstanding grass horse Halo. Halo, during his racing days and later at stud, was one surly, disagreeable, rough horse. He gave Mack many a gray hair. Halo took great pleasure each day, when sent out in one of the large Engelhard sets of trainees, in dumping his rider. He would then gallop around the track several times. His exuberance gratified, he would conclude his adventures by crossing Two Notch Road and trying to breed any and every horse that was being cooled out on the Greentree walking ring. This intrusion into the Greentree compound was quite disruptive, and annoyingly repetitive, Gaver felt.

One day, after such an episode, Gaver ran into Mack down at the clockers' stand and said, "Mack, you're going to have to take care of that son of a bitch! *Or I'm going to castrate him!*"

Since Halo became one of the best sires of his day, it is fortunate for the breed that Mack was able to control Halo's unscheduled trips to Greentree.

One of John Gaver's pet peeves was a white or flamboyantly marked stable pony. It is a fact that such animals are very disquieting to young Thoroughbred horses. Green yearlings or two-year-olds, alert to any excuse to shy or prop or raise hell generally, will invariably spook at a white or Appaloosa stable pony. Gaver would have been more favorably inclined anyway toward the more conservatively marked chestnut or bay work-animal. "Cowboy" trappings were not for him.

A rather distinguished trainer of Russian descent worked in Aiken in the fifties and sixties. He was the very continental Oleg Dubassof. Oleg had acquired a very flashy, snow-white stable pony that looked as if he had been lifted from the circus. Oleg was very proud of this beast and felt that horse and rider cut a dashing figure as they moved about the training track each morning.

Trouble was the white pony was disconcerting the hell out of the Greentree babies as they learned the rudiments of the game. This was a constant irritant to the crusty old Greentree trainer.

Finally one day Gaver could stand it no longer. When Oleg cantered proudly by, John called the Russian over. "Oleg," he asked pleasantly, "Would you consider selling me that absolutely beautiful, snow-white stable pony you're on?"

"Oh no, John, this animal would never be for sale! Why? What in the world would you do with him?" Dubassof asked.

"I'd like to kill the son of a bitch!" Gaver explained.

Since then white stable ponies in Aiken have been as abundant as statues of William Tecumseh Sherman.

Some of the great racehorses of the past sixty years, representing many illustrious trainers and outfits in our game, have "girded their loins" in winter quarters in Aiken. And they still do.

Ocala

But if Aiken tends to be aristocratic, Ocala, Florida, is blue collar, a working man's horse town and a damned good one. Never has a locale bred and trained a greater percentage of tough, hard-knocking racehorses as Ocala and surrounding

Marion County. Ocala is simply newer on the scene.

About fifty years ago, there were only a few cow ponies in Ocala when a far-sighted horseman named Carl Rose saw the possibilities of breeding and training horses in the sunny, year-round climate of Central Florida. Some others joined him, and one of them (luckily for the future of Marion County) was a former Maryland car salesman-turned-horseman. His name was Joe O'Farrell. He loved racing, "Blarney" was his middle name, and "Ocala" was his battle cry! He never stopped glorifying the virtues of raising horses on the phosphate-rich land of Marion County. His message was received. Soon that part of Florida was flourishing with horse farms and people wanting to buy racehorses. Ocala has never looked back.

Ocala doesn't have the feeling, the ambiance of Lexington or Aiken or Middleburg. It is not as tony. It is not old money, not exactly quiet, good taste, nor is it traditional. No tweed caps there but plenty of ten-gallon Stetsons! And, Ocala is a trifle "in-your-face," proud of what it has accomplished, with a right to be!

The farms are beautiful, with Spanish moss dripping from lovely, old live oaks. But the entrances may tend to be a bit more, shall we say, creative. There is a lot of Texas in Ocala, figuratively and literally. But whatever its personality, those people know how to breed, train, and develop racehorses. Ocala is still vastly underrated in our world, and statistics from the racetrack will back this up.

One of my favorite characters in the horse world happened to be a Texan transplanted to Ocala named Clayton O'Quinn, about whom numerous colorful stories abound.

Clayton, in his eighties when he died in 2001, was a good old country boy, with cowboy ways. He was a great friend, a man of spotless integrity, and a benevolent, admirable human being. He was also a man who lived by the golden rule: "Do unto others as you would have them do unto you."

But if a man violated this simple convention, in Clayton's opinion, chances were Clayton reacted by beating the living hell out of that individual. This behavioral tendency was good to remember, because Clayton was one tough customer.

In earlier days Clayton bred and sold racehorses on his own and also managed a horse farm for a gentleman from Detroit. When I first knew Clayton, he was in his late forties, weighed about two hundred pounds and was built along the lines of Jack Dempsey. Clayton stayed in fighting trim through diligent use of training equipment installed behind the house on the farm.

He dressed and looked like a rodeo bulldogger — cowboy boots, tight blue jeans, big silver belt buckle, white long-sleeved shirt with snaps, and a Stetson, of course.

Clayton had a kindly, optimistic outlook emanating from a countenance that was decidedly pleasant, but not pretty. And at such time as his expression ceased to convey complete affability, it was a clear signal that trouble was on the way. He had a sort of high, keening voice — not the sound one would associate with a man who could enthusiastically wreak heavy havoc.

In addition to horses, this man had two other interests close to his heart.

One was his family, which included his own sons and daughters, and, reportedly, more than a dozen homeless children taken in through the years and raised to be worthwhile citizens. (Under Clayton's tutelage, all of the boys and a few of the girls were required to throw leather at the heavy training bag — and at one another — in the backyard of the farm house.)

Another interest, and one that was entirely compatible with his outlook on life, was the breeding of pit bulldogs. What end uses Clayton sought for these pugnacious dogs is best left unexplored. But breed them he did, and he owned a famous pit bull named, appropriately enough, "Bully."

(My farm manager at Dogwood one Christmas presented me with a puppy that was a direct descendant of Clayton's Bully. I named this big brindled dog "Dempsey," and he was the joy of my life!)

I bought several horses from Clayton O'Quinn through the years, and he was a pleasure to do business with. When he told you something, you could "put it in the bank." And if he liked you, he put complete trust in you.

His bellicose nature, when provoked, was demonstrated vividly one day at Gulfstream Park in Florida. I had taken a consignment of horses to the Hialeah two-year-old sale, and so had O'Quinn. In those days horses for the Hialeah sales usually were housed at Gulfstream, and we were stabled in neighboring barns, connected by a paved courtyard where we both showed our horses to prospective buyers.

The afternoon of the sale, during a rather slow time, I was reared back in a camp chair outside my barn, half asleep in the sunshine. I observed a trainer I knew slightly, a rather obnoxious fellow, bearing down on Clayton's barn. The man sauntered up and asked for a certain hip number, and Clayton's people prepared and brought out this bay filly. The trainer looked at her from several angles and asked that she be walked. He then noticed that the filly had a splint, a bony growth on the inside of her cannon bone. He stared at it, noted it in his catalog, and then leaned down and squeezed it. The filly flinched sharply.

Clayton, standing nearby, said, "Yeah, she's got a splint, and it *is* tender."

That should have ended the subject of the splint, but the trainer continued to stare at her front leg and then reached down and squeezed the splint again, harder. Again she reacted from the pain.

Clayton almost whispered, "Don't touch her leg again... please, sir."

The trainer smirked at Clayton, took a step toward the filly, bent over, and…

That's all she wrote!

Clayton grabbed him by the shoulder, tore half the man's shirt off, and knocked him halfway across the tarmac work area.

The terrified filly got loose from her showman. But no matter. Clayton was on his man like Dempsey after Tunney. The trainer struggled to his feet. And that was another in a series of mistakes he had committed in the span of a few minutes. Clayton came from deep center field with a right cross.

Outside my barn I had placed a large, wooden sandwich board, on which were displayed the hip numbers and breeding of the horses I was selling. Clayton knocked that trainer into my sandwich board and produced kindling. By that time the starting-gate crew, waiting for the next six-furlong race just outside the tall hedge that separated the barns from the racetrack, and several of us from my barn got a hold of Clayton, and the melee was over. After a few minutes of very heavy breathing, the prospective buyer struggled away from the area.

Clayton came over to my barn later, smiling sheepishly, and in his high voice said, "I want to make it up to you for ruining your sign."

"Clayton, do not give it a second thought," I said.

I really don't know who bought Clayton's filly that night, but I don't believe it was the gentleman who was so concerned with her splint.

The man whose farm Clayton managed for a number of years kept at it until he was in the neighborhood of one hundred years of age — and for a while, understandably, he had not been at the top of his game, judgment-wise. As was his perfect right, he was given to making deals on stud seasons. Often these deals did not make sense. Clayton was caught in the middle of these cockamamie transactions, and since he liked the old man — and it was his job — he struggled constantly with "damage control."

At one point the old fellow purchased from a breeder in Kentucky a "no-guarantee season" to one of the most glamorous stallions of that era. This means that the money was paid up front, and if the mare did not get in foal, for *any* reason, the money was blown.

The old man advised Clayton of this transaction and instructed him to ship a certain mare to the breeder's farm in Lexington. Clayton, of course, complied, though he was unenthusiastic about the efficacy of the arrangement.

Clayton phoned the breeder periodically during the spring to determine if and when the mare had been bred to the stud. The communications were unsatisfactory, and the few answers that were supplied were not pleasing to Clayton. Mid-April came and the mare was not in foal. It was reported that she had not come in heat, and, therefore, she had not been covered. Clayton began to fret seriously. He feared the season would go by and (1) the good mare would not be impregnated; furthermore, (2) his somewhat befuddled patron would lose the significant "no guarantee" fee.

One day in late April, Clayton called the breeder and asked, "What about our mare? How come she hasn't been bred? We need to know what's going on."

According to Clayton, this was the reply: "Don't worry about it; I'm going to get it done! It's none of your business, anyway. You're just the goddamned farm manager!"

Long pause. Clayton hung up. Then he made another call. He rang down to his own broodmare barn. When his man answered, Clayton instructed, "Bubba, get the small van ready. We're going to take a trip to Kentucky."

Bubba and Clayton drove all night from Ocala to Lexington. Clayton was not in a conversational mood.

The next morning they rolled through the gates of the farm and stopped at the office to determine the head man's whereabouts and were told that he was down at the yearling barn. That became their immediate destination.

Clayton descended on the unfortunate yearling barn with the fervor of Attila the Hun. Suffice it to say, not long afterward, when he and Bubba departed in the van with the mare on board, the atmosphere on that farm was like that of Atlanta after Sherman laid waste to it.

There was a significant financial adjustment on this breeding arrangement, and the mare was impregnated by another stallion, though quite late in the season.

The last time I saw Clayton's son, he shook his head in admiration and relayed the following story. Not long before Clayton died "he was in a little country store, and he wanted to buy a cold drink. He was bent over rooting around in the bottom of this old-time cooler, trying to find a ginger ale or something. This young farm worker was behind my dad, waiting to get himself a drink, and he got impatient. He said, 'Come on, Pop, pick one out!' Clayton glanced back at him and then kept on looking for the drink he wanted. The guy in a big hurry waited another thirty seconds and then yelled out, 'Move it, grandpa!' and nudged him in the back pretty hard. Clayton came whirling out of that drink box and decked him.

"Now the fellow is lying in between some empty cases of drinks, moaning, and holding his bloody nose. The proprietor came running over and said, 'What's happening here?'

"Clayton glanced down at his victim, looked kinda puzzled, and said, 'Oh, my goodness! He must have fell down.' "

Franklin

A good five hundred miles lies between Ocala, Florida, and Franklin, Tennessee — a significant span geographically and also in appearance and personality.

Franklin and Williamson County — just south of Nashville — were not strangers to the horse. At one point in this nation's history, middle Tennessee was the hotbed of horse racing in America. (Remember Andrew Jackson? He was the August Belmont of several centuries ago.)

When I came there with my family more than sixty years ago, the area teemed with Thoroughbreds, Saddle Horses, Walking Horses, and Arabians. Such prominent racing personalities as Smiser West, Henry Forrest, George Sloan, Calvin Houghland, DeWitt Owen, and Tennessee Wright have been associated with that region.

Logic has nothing whatsoever to do with how my family got to Franklin. But logic and my father were not always running mates. He had abruptly sold his interest in his Coca-Cola bottling plant in Des Moines, Iowa, vacated the presidency thereof, bought a farm in middle Tennessee, and decided, by God, to go into the racehorse business. It was 1940.

During his entire life my father had been either up or down. He was now about to embrace a "down" from which he would never recover — economically. But the establishment of Shoestring Farm ("started on a shoestring," that was for sure) was a project loaded with derring-do, if nothing else. Strong drink played an important role in his divorcing himself from the ever-so-bountiful Coke franchise, and certainly in his subsequent purchase for $18,500 (pretty big money in 1940) of a lovely, if run-down, farm, with a spectacular antebellum home as the keystone of the operation. It was an absolutely nonsensical thing to do. My father was going to support his family — in his typically high-on-the-hog manner — with income from Thoroughbred racehorses. Somehow. I don't know whether he intended to do this through betting on them, breeding them, winning purses with them, or a combination of all three. Nor did he know. He would figure it out as he went along — the way he had done a lot of things, some of them very successfully.

Much to the delight of that sleepy little community of two thousand horse-oriented souls, the 112 acres of the new Shoestring Farm were literally churning with construction activity. A huge barn was being built, a half-mile racetrack was under construction, white board fences were going up, and "the big house" was undergoing refurbishing and being decorated to the nines.

Reeking of history and glorious tradition, Franklin was a lovely little town in those days, eighteen miles south of Nashville. The farmland there is rich and luxuriant with outcroppings of limestone rock, like in Kentucky. Franklin's economy in 1940 depended entirely on agriculture — horses and mules, various food crops, and tobacco. As a result, the town was quiet through the week but swarming with activity on Saturday, when farmers, some modest and some quite substantial, came to town with their families to trade, shop, listen to the leather-lunged street preachers around the square, shoot pool, talk about horses, and/or get drunk.

In those days one often saw a team of workhorses trotting down Main Street with the farmer at the reins and his family spilling over the sides of the wagon. They would do their shopping and gossiping at the dry goods, feed, hardware, or grocery stores. Then the children might be deposited at the picture show and the wife would find a little visiting to do. The head of the house and maybe the oldest boy would settle in at Ham's Pool Room, strategically situated on the square between West Point Grill and Baker Lane's Barber Shop (where, for some special reason, there hung a tremendous painting of Johnstown winning the Derby). This portion of town was an environment of conviviality. And, bookmakers had been known to stroll into Ham's when the big races were coming up in Louisville, New Orleans, or New York. And they weren't looking for a pool game.

By 1943 the Campbells' days in Franklin were numbered. Doomed was the Shoestring Farm dream, launched with such enthusiasm by my father and so exciting to me. It was now becoming a ghastly nightmare. This Thoroughbred racing venture with the decidedly muddled marketing plan had little shot for survival under the finest conditions, and in 1941 with the outbreak of World War II, its hopes were obliterated.

My father had broodmares producing foals. Horses were campaigning at Oaklawn Park, Churchill Downs, and Detroit Race Track. Young horses were being broken and trained on our recently completed racetrack. None of this made an iota of economic sense in the early days of the war.

When the United States entered the war, many racetracks were closed as "non-essential wartime activities." Gasoline was rationed, and it was almost impossible to transport horses. In fact, by the time 1942 was half over, you literally would have had a hard time *giving* a horse to someone. You sure as hell could not sell one!

The contractors and suppliers who produced the splendid barn, laid out the racetrack, and put up all those white fences had not been fully paid. Because the Campbell family and their grandiose plans in this little community had seemed unquestionably solid and substantial, the creditors had not pressed aggressively for payment. But now the Shoestring operation was known to be financially very shaky. To add to the problem, it was pretty well established that my father was drinking heavily. Things were understandably getting nasty, and lawyers were becoming involved.

It didn't take long for this situation to evolve into a sale on the courthouse steps of the entire farm and all the belongings on it.

3

Drinking and Drinkers

So ended my personal chapter in the horse town of Franklin, Tennessee. I learned about a lot of things there — other than horses — and one topic in particular interested me.

I was introduced to beer and wine at age thirteen, quickly got the hang of it, and graduated to more serious stuff. When I joined the U.S. Navy in 1944, on the day I became seventeen, I think I knew I was a strong candidate for alcoholism. My addiction to strong drink steadily intensified. Until my thirtieth year.

On the night of December 7, 1957, after drinking steadily for ten days, I could take it no more. I stood for a half-hour in misting rain outside a large Atlanta hotel and thought about the absolute horror of my life. I went inside to a phone booth, called Alcoholics Anonymous and then walked twelve blocks to the AA clubhouse.

From that night to the present, I have never touched any form of alcohol. Nor have I even considered it. I had just as soon have a nice glass of strychnine! However, I have thought, after some horribly disappointing afternoons at the racetrack, if I *were* able to drink, now would be a pretty damned good time to have a big, stiff belt — maybe about four fingers in a washtub!

I immersed myself in the wonderful AA program, going frequently to meetings, sometimes several in a day. With no car or money, I did nothing but work and go to AA meetings. After several months of sobriety and dedication to my work, my dramatic turnaround was the talk of the advertising agency where I was employed. My career skyrocketed.

Deeply in debt, I steadily paid off every dollar I owed over the next few years. Never having known anything but a drinking life, I suddenly discovered a wonderful existence.

I am not proud of the fact that I am an alcoholic, but neither am I ashamed of it. Some wonderful people are alcoholics! However, I *am* proud of the fact that, with the helping hand of AA, I did have the courage to change the things that could be changed.

I have not broadcast my alcoholism and the tumult that it brought to my early days, but I have had no inclination to hide it. Indeed, I have been quite open about it. The result is that I have helped and given hope to a number of men and women beset with the same malady. I am plenty proud of this.

This is a subject that embarrasses some people. Admitting alcoholism is to them like announcing that you are a pedophile. I have also found that it irritates a few — usually people who are drinking too much, know it, but won't admit it to themselves.

In spirit, I am a member of the "drinking fraternity." I identify with drinking people. When I drank, I liked the way it tasted. I liked the way it made me feel. I liked the people I drank it with and the places where it was drunk.

For forty-four years now my life has been led in a manner that — if not exactly in the exemplary category — has at least been quite satisfactory, I believe. Consequently, I have no problem whatsoever in looking back and relating some of the decidedly roguish, outrageous, hilarious escapades of my drinking days. It is as if I were a spectator observing another man's peccadilloes.

I think I had best deal primarily with my own stories and not take liberties with other hard-drinking (active and inactive), well-known figures in the horse world. I have no business imposing my own out-of-the-closet philosophy on them. They may want to stay in the closet. We will touch gently on a couple who wouldn't mind.

Because of the effects of John Barleycorn, many people have misplaced their automobiles. However, none could ever come close to my 1955 career highlight, a shoo-in for the *Guinness Book of World Records.*

At that time I was the proud owner of a rather rakish pink Packard. It was a huge automobile, had some age on it, and I had purchased it for $325.

One night in Atlanta while out painting the town red, I motored to one of my favorite watering holes. I parked some distance away in a spot that would accommodate my rather unwieldy Packard and strode off to the bar for a period of conviviality.

I emerged around 1:30 a.m. in a confused state of mind and was unable to recall the location of the pink Packard. It was necessary to go home in a taxi. When I awakened later that morning, the whereabouts of the vehicle still eluded me. I went to work on the bus.

At the end of a trying workday, I was badly in need of a liquid restorative. I spent an hour or two taking care of that matter, then decided I had better find the Packard. Obviously, I needed transportation in order to be able to conduct the search. I was forced to go to Avis to rent a car. At this point I was in the Avis vehicle, driving around looking for the lost car. But the search was being conducted in a leisurely way with frequent relaxation breaks for cocktails. Truthfully, the location of the Packard was not an urgent motivation for my ramblings. Although I would certainly have been pleased if I had come upon the car.

Around 11 p.m. I dropped into one of my favorite haunts. And wouldn't you know! When the evening drew to a late, late close, even the location of the Avis car — whose appearance was not stamped indelibly on my mind — had slipped from my memory.

I caught a ride home, then began the next day nervously wracking my brain about the location of both the pink Packard *and* the Avis car. Alas, I could come up with no answers.

About mid-morning I made it into work, struggled through another horrible day, and determined that I simply *must* find the two cars. However, I needed yet another source of transportation to do so.

Where now would I turn?

Hertz!

Presto! Soon I was cruising about the city in a sparkling new Hertz rental car, looking for both cars, and somewhat more concerned than the night before because the situation was clearly becoming critical. I had to find these cars! In those days I was not aware of a National or Budget or Enterprise, so I was really going to be stymied if the Hertz transportation was not up to the task.

So unsettling was the predicament that I felt strongly the need for a quiet drink to soothe jangled nerves!

I whipped into a popular bar called Mammy's Shanty, where many of the pals could invariably be found. Indeed a convivial group awaited me. We ordered up several rounds of Old Grandad and water while I outlined my problems and enlisted their aid in a game plan for vehicle recovery.

With a task force that included several autos, an eager force deployed into strategic neighborhoods in search of the errant automobiles. Disappointingly though, my cohorts soon became bored with this quest and all save me called it a night.

I drove on to a favorite late-night hangout called The Blue Lantern and sought solace at the bar. When the barkeep finally called "time," I teetered out onto the sidewalk in a foggy state, and — you guessed it! — could not recall where I had parked the Hertz car!

Another cab home, then another dreadful, next-morning memory search that yielded nothing. Now I did have a very significant dilemma on my hands. At this point, I enlisted the aid of a rather levelheaded friend who could always be called upon in emergencies. I called into my office "sick" (by no means an exaggeration!), and we meticulously sought to re-create (with no alcohol to aid us) my wanderings over the past three nights. We sought the input of some confederates and several bartenders who had been with or observed me during these periods, and then we set out to locate the cars.

When the sun finally got over the yardarm that day, we had located and checked in the two rental cars, and I was in proud possession of my pink Packard.

Bringing to closure this entire exhausting ordeal, was, of course, cause for another celebration!

French Quarter Days

In my late twenties, while living in New Orleans' storied old French Quarter, I took every opportunity to attend racing at the Fair Grounds. There were three grand old handicap stars campaigning there in those days. Their names were Bobby Brocato, Spur On, and Epic King, and now it seems that almost every Saturday they took turns beating one another. Rarely did I miss being on hand when they did battle.

This was before the days of Sunday racing, thankfully for my struggling career. Sunday was my busiest day as radio-TV director of a medium-sized advertising agency in that city.

When Bauerlein Advertising Agency hired me, they stressed that the agency had charge accounts at all the leading restaurants and bars in the city and that part of my job description would include the entertainment of major clients and prospective clients. I assured them they had found the right man for the job! This directive was similar to throwing Brer Rabbit into the briar patch!

One of my many non-entertainment chores was the production (in every sense of the word) of a TV cooking show. It aired at the very strange time of one o'clock on Sunday afternoons.

It was sponsored by Agar Hams, Lou-Anna Salad Oil, and Dulaney Frozen Vegetables. It was up to me to see to it that each of these products was demonstrated temptingly every Sunday from one to one-thirty. On Sunday mornings I had to devise and prepare a scrumptious culinary presentation for each product, take the dishes to the studio, and see that they were attractively displayed for the camera. The announcer who was going to enthuse over the products had to be rehearsed by me (the director) and then the show was aired. Why anyone would have watched it, I do not know, but I suppose they did.

The title of radio-TV director for this advertising agency meant that I was almost literally the "chief cook and bottle washer" for anything that fell within the realm of these two media.

The events of one Sunday almost brought about the unraveling of my career in the New Orleans advertising world. Actually the causation came on the Saturday night before.

I lived in an apartment in the French Quarter. Given my primary recreation, this dwelling was ideally situated, because it placed me close to about fifty serious drinking establishments.

That Saturday night I had "tied one on," dividing my enthusiastic patronage among the Absinthe House Bar, The Famous Door, and Court of Two Sisters. After a very full (in every sense of the word) evening, I had fallen wearily into the "arms of Morpheus" and slept quite soundly until around nine on Sunday morning.

I had a horrendous hangover. After dressing hurriedly, I gamely addressed the preparation of the featured attractions of the upcoming cooking show, now about three hours away. I made a rather anemic-looking tossed salad onto which we would later pour the "zesty Lou-Anna French Dressing." I then cooked some of the "plump and tender" Dulaney fordhook lima beans. Finally, I unwrapped the Agar Ham, scored ragged-looking diamonds into it, and ran it into my antiquated oven for ninety minutes of baking.

My hangover had not improved one whit after these exertions. I had a terrible thirst, and my mental outlook on the upcoming day was dreadfully bleak. Suddenly, a wonderful thought entered my head. The ham was cooking away, and I had an adequate "window of opportunity" before heading to the nearby studio on Royal Street, so why did I not repair to one of my favorite neighboring bars. I chose Lafitte's Blacksmith Shop and went there to have a nice bracer in the form of a Ramos Gin Fizz. This drink, made with the white of an egg, would serve as both a nutritious breakfast and, more importantly, a badly needed restorative.

My enthusiasm, moments before in such short supply, now had returned and within minutes I was seated at Lafitte's bar having my first one. It went down easily, and before long I was working on my second. Soon other convivial souls came into the popular bar, and I found myself seated at a table with some of the pals. We were having a splendid time, reliving the events of the previous night and making plans for upcoming entertainment. The morning was now going swimmingly.

The delightful mood of the occasion was slightly altered, however, when a fire engine, its siren wide open, came careering up Bourbon Street. But we paid little attention.

Within minutes, another big fire truck came clamoring past the bar. Now we began to be interested in the fire's location. I glanced out the window, and, oh my God, it became crystal clear! Smoke could be seen billowing out of an apartment down on Ursulines Street. *My* apartment! The damned ham, now cooking for over two hours, was on fire!

I sprinted homeward, rushed through the courtyard, bounded up the steps (the firemen following my lead), and groped my way into the smoke-filled kitchen. I flung open the oven door, at which point a fireman unleashed his portable extinguisher onto the flaming ham. The crisis was over.

However, the ham now appeared jet-black and was severely shriveled. The Agar people would not be pleased.

The firemen found it necessary to ask a few rather rude questions (they were in a most disgruntled mood when they discovered the cause of the blaze). The landlady, who had turned in the alarm, hovered nearby, adding considerably to the distinctly disputatious nature of the gathering. By the time they had all dispersed, midst serious warnings to me, airtime for the cooking show was dangerously close. And here am I with a ham that looked as if it had been nuked, a very sooty salad, and lima beans that have turned charcoal gray.

I scraped and doctored up the ham carcass as best I could, poured Coca-Cola over it (having learned that this gave it a succulent, healthy appearance on camera), and with my other dishes on a huge tray, I set off for WDSU-TV about six blocks away. I was on foot.

This took place in February, the season for Mardi Gras parades. It had slipped my mind that a big one was scheduled for 11 a.m. that Sunday. It was sure to be hitting its best stride on Royal Street in the heart of the French Quarter just about now. It was.

The floats came by in close-order drill, with barricades set up on the sidewalks to hold back pedestrians. There I stood after a disastrous morning now cruelly thwarted from reaching my destination with that which was entirely necessary to stage the cooking show.

Sweating profusely while holding my fifteen-pound tray, I pleaded with a policeman to get me across. No dice.

Finally a passable gap in the parade opened, and I darted across. I arrived at the studio in just the nick of time.

The smart-ass announcer who would soon gush charmingly about the ham, beans, and salad, looked warily at the foodstuffs, then at me, and said, "All of you look like you've been dragged through a keyhole!"

We went on the air, and, while I sweated it, there were no repercussions. After all, who would be watching a cooking show on television at one o'clock in the afternoon during Mardi Gras.

Candidates for Substance Abuse

Drinkers come from every walk of life and every element of society, with no clear-cut pattern of shared characteristics. But "occupational profiling" would substantiate that men and women who reside in the racing world, where the envelope is pushed much of the time and hopes and dreams are worn on sleeves (and constantly brushed off), are prime substance abuse candidates.

Every industry has people who think its operating conditions are uniquely difficult and excessively challenging, and each field does have its own unique problems. As one who has toiled in various forms of commerce and industry, and has been in a position to observe many more, I state that horse racing is in a class by itself when the degree of difficulty for success is cranked into the equation!

So, if one breeds, owns, trains, rides, or even grooms horses, strong drink or drugs provide a powerful lure when seeking relief from the constant pressure to succeed.

What better group to be tempted than jockeys? While some do not know the meaning of fear, most do. And they are justified. Their livelihood is exceedingly dangerous. Most riders must starve themselves and resort to other barbaric practices to keep their weight under control. This would not contribute to one's peace of mind.

The necessity of success, of course, is unquestionable. Yet how do you succeed unless you can ride the best horses? But you won't ride them until you prove that you can win on some that are not the best. And when you get to the point that your services are in demand for the good stock, you'd better not make any mistakes. Think about this: who is most conveniently blamed for a losing effort on an 8-5 shot?

Wouldn't you find it tempting to snort a few lines of coke or take on a load of vodka?

It is interesting that a trio of the greatest, highest-profile riders of the last part of the twentieth century struggled with this problem, licked it, and went public with their dependency. And in the process — God bless them — they have helped many another poor soul who has lost control of his life.

They are Pat Day, Jerry Bailey, and from England, Walter Swinburn.

One of my all-time favorite characters in racing was Warner Jones, once described as one-third snake oil salesman, one-third riverboat gambler, and one-third Southern gentleman. Rudyard Kipling, in his great poem "If," referred to one who has "walked with kings but has not lost the common touch." That was Warner.

He was a drinking man's drinker in his early days. When he had achieved "world-class" status, he quit drinking. He credited AA with helping him turn his life around, and he helped hundreds of others by introducing them to the twelve-step program of Alcoholics Anonymous. One of those disciples was Tom Meeker, president of Churchill Downs and one of the most respected figures on the Thoroughbred racing scene today. And so was Warner a stalwart in the Thoroughbred industry.

Warner was to the manor born. His background included several of the most prominent families in Louisville. All he ever wanted to do with the early part of his life was to raise hell, and breed and race horses. This program was not necessarily incompatible with a background of wealth and position in the state of Kentucky. Warner did all of the above with superb efficiency.

Later he would help create the American Horse Council, co-found and serve as director of one of Kentucky's biggest banking institutions, breed a Kentucky Derby winner (Dark Star), and become chairman of the board of Churchill Downs. He was one of Kentucky's most respected citizens.

But in his younger, incorrigible days he was a "stem-winder." And incidents like this one at the Louisville Country Club earned him that reputation. It is still talked about today when the subject of either the man or the club comes up. The story has numerous versions, but this one happens to be my favorite.

As a horseman, Warner had access to certain veterinary supplies; and as a socialite he was often an enthusiastic participant in the social functions of the fine, old Louisville club. These two aspects of his life came together in a most unfortunate way one summer evening many years ago.

Warner felt that the atmosphere of most social occasions at the club was considerably more restrained than he found stimulating. And so when the annual Summer Members Ball rolled around, Warner decided it would be amusing to introduce some energizer to what was usually a rather routine, run-of-the-mill dance.

Once the guests had arrived and the festivities had hit full stride — dreadfully tame though that be, in Warner's view — young Mr. Jones sauntered past the enormous punch bowl and casually dropped in not one — but *three* — physic balls.

Now, a physic ball is an object about the size of a small golf ball, and it was — in yesteryear — a large-animal purgative, a laxative. This gigantic pill would promptly and forcefully eliminate even the most severe form of constipation in an 1,100-pound horse. Three of them would alleviate the clogged bowels of an entire herd of elephants. You can imagine the effect it had on the human celebrants that evening at the Louisville Country Club.

I do not know whether Warner ever confessed to the deed, or he was seen spiking the punch by another guest, or some conscience-stricken accessory to the fact sounded the alarm. At any rate, the party broke up unusually early that particular evening; guests began to recognize the unmistakable signals that Warner had envisioned. Many departed hurriedly, feeling that they might be better able to deal with the consequences of the physic balls in the privacy of their own homes.

It is known that Warner was identified with that year's very unsuccessful Summer Members Ball.

I believe he was granted a lengthy "leave of absence" from the club.

Albert Warner

One of my horse partners of yesteryear was an absolutely delightful man from Birmingham named Albert Warner. When we first met, he had weathered sixty-five action-packed years. But Father Time had not allowed gravity to burden his outlook on life. He approached life as he had when a sophomore at the Sigma Alpha Epsilon house at Auburn.

Albert liked to drink, did drink, and, if the truth be told, could not have gotten along very well without it. But he was fun, stayed on a pretty even keel, and we were really devoted friends. He knew I talked the same language.

Albert was a sports fan par excellence. And he loved horse racing. He invested in some of our horses and had the time of his life doing it. He liked to win, but mostly he liked to travel to the races to see them run, and he would use these occasions to kick up his heels.

Albert came from a well-connected but impecunious Birmingham family. As a young man he was very popular, good looking, and athletic. These attributes let him marry into a very wealthy Alabama family and subsequently rise to the presidency of a small company in Birmingham. I do not think it was the most complex of the family's diverse stable of businesses.

His wife was an attractive, strong-willed lady. She adored her husband but recognized his shortcomings and was concerned lest they be permitted to get out of hand. As a result, Albert was kept on a rather short leash at home. Thus, he welcomed the opportunity to travel.

And travel he did. If we ran one of his horses — or anybody's horse — in Miami, New Orleans, Louisville, or New York (his favorite cities, in that order), he needed to be on hand to evaluate the "conservation of his property."

Albert was a riot. But he could cause problems.

I remember well an incident in Miami. We were running a colt at Gulfstream one day, and Albert had elected to come down, although I had made it clear that the colt would "need a race." Truth is Albert needed a race even more than the colt did. He flew down to Ft. Lauderdale the afternoon before, and because it was in the height of the season, he had trouble finding lodging. He was not very particular, so he settled for a room in a rather sleazy motel, on Federal Highway, right across from the entrance to Gulfstream.

We ran the colt — and he did need the race! Despite warnings that he would, Albert had wagered a significant amount on him. So he was not in his usual jolly frame of mind when he left Gulfstream to walk across the busy thoroughfare — during five o'clock traffic. As the still nimble Albert dodged his way through the creeping lanes of traffic, one grumpy motorist blew his horn at him.

"Kiss my ass!" Albert screamed sweetly.

This response evoked a crude gesture and some uncomplimentary remarks from the driver, who was perhaps emboldened by the target's obviously advanced years.

In a bad mood to begin with, Albert was enraged, and with the offending car at a standstill in the stalled traffic, he headed in that direction.

Wisely, the motorist sensed that the situation was becoming more complicated than he desired. He raised his window and locked his doors.

Albert sought unsuccessfully to gain admittance to the vehicle whose occupant had insulted him. His only recourse seemed to be to stand by the door and scream unpleasant threats at the motorist (who was now exceedingly anxious for the flow of traffic to unclog). The driver simply stared stoically ahead, trying to pretend that this deranged man did not exist.

Suddenly, Albert conceived a very creative idea, which he immediately implemented.

Realizing that he was wearing shoes with hard leather heels, Albert untied one, removed it, and — in the middle of U.S. 1 (Federal Highway) — began to destroy the side window on this gentleman's automobile.

I happened to be leaving the racetrack about this time and observed the ruckus. I could see that my friend Albert was heavily involved. I whipped into a nearby gas station and rushed over to the melee.

When I came up, Albert had finished pulverizing the window and was intent on dragging the driver from the car through the jagged remains. The seat belt seemed to be the only thing standing in the way!

The traffic police at Gulfstream had come upon the scene,

and we were about to encounter a very sticky wicket, indeed. At this point all concerned — save Albert — were anxious to go on about their business, and, with some slight encouraging on my part, we were able to "bring closure" to this troublesome affair.

Albert Warner liked to lunch at the racetrack. Actually, what he liked was to drink two or three martinis, followed by the mastication of fifty percent of a shrimp cocktail.

If we were running a horse in a later race, Albert might arrive on the premises in a slightly nervous frame of mind. This could result in a heightened appetite for martinis. His post-prandial procedure might then be to disappear for a bit. He wanted more to drink, but he felt that I would quickly recognize this as an unacceptably unorthodox drinking pattern. Often this practice would result in Albert's becoming confused as to post-time for his horse's race. He might not show up in the paddock, for the viewing of the race, or even for winner's circle ceremonies.

It was this eventuality that presented grave consequences for Albert. Here's why:

The winner's circle photo would be made, but Albert's smiling face would not be among the celebrants (because he was in some bar on the racetrack premises). The photos would be processed, our office would order prints for the partners, and Albert's would be sent to his home (an unseemly subject matter for the office, the family felt).

Mrs. Warner, a lady of considerable curiosity when it came to Albert's activities, would often open the envelope from Dogwood. She would study the victory photo with great interest.

But why was Albert not there?

The first time Albert was able to cook up some absurd rationale for his absence. However, when Mrs. Warner encountered this strange circumstance for the second time, she logically wanted to know, "Where in the hell have you *been*, Albert?"

There was no logical answer but the truth, and admitting he had had so much to drink that he had missed the race did not sit well with "the little lady."

He realized this could not be permitted to happen again or travel might be severely restricted. And realistically he knew he was not likely to mend his ways. Albert devised a clever solution.

First, he advised our office to send the win pictures to his office, not his home. He knew his wife would still inquire about, and wish to view, the pictures, so there had to be a more complex element to the scheme.

One day Albert got himself dolled up in his usual blue blazer, gray flannel slacks racetrack garb and went to a photography studio near his office in Birmingham.

Striking a jaunty, celebratory pose some twenty feet from the camera, Albert directed the photographer to shoot.

This image of the smiling, jubilant owner was kept secretly in the studio. In the future, whenever Albert was lucky enough to win a race (but not make the winner's circle), the photographer would simply secure from Albert the track photographer's official picture, and then he would superimpose Albert onto the group. And shoot it again.

Sometimes, depending on the size, composition, or body language of the group, the result could be flawed. But it worked passably. Mrs. Warner was not interested in scrutinizing the picture, once she had ascertained that Albert was "tending to business." The fact that Albert sometimes seemed to be levitating escaped her.

4

Life in the Horse Business

A dog, not a horse, was the highlight of the 1984 Washington, D.C., International. This race was run for many years at Laurel Race Course and was one of the great races of its day. Conceived by John Shapiro, Laurel's owner, the invitational grass race at a mile and a half attracted the stellar turf runners of every major racing nation.

The International flourished until the Breeders' Cup was established. Its timing (around November 1) conflicted head-on with what is today known as the World Thoroughbred Championships. A clash with the long-established major turf fixtures in New York prevented it from being rescheduled. So it died a natural death.

Dogwood ran in it in 1984 with Nassipour, and the night before the event a screamingly funny situation occurred at the Canadian Embassy.

John Shapiro glamorized his race marvelously by surrounding it with glittering parties. It was a highlight of Washington's fall social season. Usually one of the major embassies hosted a beautiful dinner. In 1984 Canada did the honors.

Washington was seriously cold that weekend, unfortunate because the party's large size necessitated the erection of a tent for the dinner portion of the party. Cocktails were served inside in the lovely embassy foyer.

Anne and I and our Dogwood partners were bowled over

by the gorgeous party and its extremely elegant setting. And we were charmed when we observed the ambassador's family dog, a tremendous Russian wolfhound, wandering amiably among the distinguished guests during the cocktail hour.

This was a very appealing, "down home" touch to what otherwise could have been a rather stuffy affair.

Ambassadors whose countries had entrants in the race were all present. That year, Russia — despite the chilly Cold War relationship with the United States — was represented with a horse in the International. That country's envoy was present, and he definitely looked the part. He was tall and spare, with prominent features supporting a huge, but very patrician, nose. He had a luxuriant head of wiry gray hair that swept back in wild profusion from a high, pallid, blue-veined forehead. He looked like a mad scientist or a symphony conductor.

The dinner hour was announced, and we filed apprehensively into the uncomfortable climate of the tent (we are talking cold!). Space heaters blew hot air throughout the spacious tent, and the embassy staff actually handed out thermal socks — to put over our shoes — as we went in.

Our table for ten happened to be adjacent to the Russian ambassador's, and we watched with interest as this stork of a man stalked somberly past us. He was clad in a dramatic, floor-length fur coat, ideal for Russian winters and not a bad idea for this night in Washington. After removing and draping the coat over the back of the chair, he seated himself.

The congenial family dog had also strolled in with the other guests. Undaunted by the frigid conditions, he had reclined between the two tables to await the evening's proceedings.

The meal was served, the wine replenished generously, and the party was going nicely, considering the temperature.

After dessert and coffee, the Canadian ambassador rose to toast the fine horses that would face the starter on the morrow.

He then remarked on the great, healing significance of friendly competition at the International at a time in Cold War history when relations between many nations were tenuous.

The Russian ambassador decided at this juncture that he was cold, and he shrugged himself into his great fur coat.

With that, the huge dog, dozing several feet away, jolted to attention. He jumped up and stood riveted by this heretofore unobserved large, hairy object. His head was lowered like that of a bull before a charge.

Inexplicably, this animal (who stood a good six feet when on his back legs) leapt onto the back of the unsuspecting diplomat, planted his front legs on the man's shoulders, and began — with astounding enthusiasm — to make love to this irresistibly attractive, furry creature.

Thrusting rhythmically and vigorously, with a seriously rapt demeanor about him, this dog now completely stole the attention of the entire party. The host began to falter slightly in his remarks, but could hardly stop and scream at his "pet." He had no choice but to continue gamely.

But the "mother of all dilemmas" lay with the Russian ambassador; never would his skills of diplomacy be so severely tested.

First, he looked around with some understandable surprise to ascertain the nature of the attack. When he had assessed the situation, he addressed the problem by shrugging his shoulders discouragingly, glaring menacingly at the beast, while uttering a sharp but well-modulated command. It did not work.

The huge wolfhound picked up the tempo, if anything.

What a problem! The ambassador must bring closure to this unseemly episode. The speaker was by now just going through the motions; the audience was tittering audibly, and some members were in stitches! Everyone in the tent was aware of this humiliating spectacle.

The ambassador had several choices, none of them promising.

He could get up and walk out. But this was fraught with risk. He couldn't be sure just what the response of the Russian wolfhound might be. Would this stimulate him further? How would it play that a high-ranking diplomat was vanquished from the field by the amorous attentions of a large dog!

He could turn and smite the dog forcefully, sending a signal that this activity was not at all suitable for this occasion. But, we're talking here about a very, very large dog, in a most intense frame of mind. Would this be a judicious course of action? Of considerably less significance at this point, the animal was the house pet of the host (who would have cheerfully slit the animal's throat right about then!).

Third, he could try removing the garment that triggered all this misery in the first place.

The Russian did take off the coat, struggling mightily and trying not to stand up and attract further attention while he did so. He then tossed the troublesome garment several feet away between the tables. This did the trick.

The dog reluctantly dismounted and looked completely crestfallen. He stared first at the now inanimate fur coat, then at the seething ambassador. Had he been able to shrug his shoulders as if to say, "Well, it was nice while it lasted," he would have done so. He then lay down to resume his nap.

By this time the party was in complete chaos. Midst audible giggling, the host lamely finished his lofty remarks. We clapped politely, adjourned, and headed for valet parking, with the Russian ambassador leading the way.

The race the next day was wonderful as always (Dogwood was fourth), but it was decidedly anticlimactic.

The Dogwood Arab

In the mid-eighties the great Arab sheikhs invaded Kentucky. They came to the sales, bringing with them crusty old British bloodstock advisers, great determination, and untold millions of dollars with which to do damage. They were loaded for bear. The three Maktoum brothers from the United Arab Emirates, along with Saudi Arabia's Prince Khalid Abdullah and Mahmoud Fustok, and other lesser lights with monikers too complicated and similar to attempt, came to buy the cream of each year's crop.

The major sales companies, every consignor, indeed any human being with aspirations of making money in the horse industry, wanted a piece of "the Arabs."

I decided it would be great fun if Dogwood manufactured its very own Arab.

I should interject here that I have always been a sucker for a midget. I love midgets. I think there is no situation that can't be enlivened by the judicious involvement of a midget!

Once, in an earlier life, when I was chairman of an advertising agency in Atlanta, I hired a midget, dressed him as a Western Union delivery boy (an unheard-of occupation today), and had him deliver an oversized telegram to a prospective client we were pitching. It didn't work, but it wasn't the midget's fault!

Now, in a very whimsical spoof, designed to do nothing but entertain ourselves — and, hopefully, a lot of other people in the horse world — we created "Sheikh Bin Had" (Bin Had, get it?).

The role of the sheikh was played by a midget — in real life an undersized bellman employed by the Hilton Hotel in Atlanta. We hired this gentleman (he stood all of four feet), fitted him in loose-flowing Arabic garb, with burnoose, and set up a photo session at Dogwood Farm, our 433-acre training farm near Columbus, Georgia.

We arranged a stretch limousine and the sheikh motored to the farm, in costume, of course. He was driven there by his bodyguard-driver, "Punjab."

Dogwood farm manager Ron Stevens and I were there to greet Bin Had, and the cameras started clicking. We brought horses out on our racetrack for training; the sheikh inspected them, and we looked others over in the paddock. After several hours we had photographically captured everything a visiting potentate might logically do on a Thoroughbred horse farm.

We then fashioned a news story for our Dogwood Farm quarterly newsletter. The gist of it was that Sheikh Bin Had had come to America to buy shares in horses from Dogwood.

The front page bannered this headline:

"Arab Potentate goes wild on Christmas Shopping Spree! DOGWOOD HORSE INVENTORY DEPLETED!"

The body copy read: "Dogwood Farm, one of the few commercial thoroughbred operations in America without a tie to Arabic petrodollars, has now catapulted to the top of the heap following an epic equine Christmas shopping spree by Sheikh Bin Had.

"Sheikh Bin Had, known as 'The Desert Mouse,' visited Dogwood in his never-ending quest to acquire unique gifts to please his 27 wives. Lest any of his wives take exception should one horse do better than another, 27 horses were packaged into a limited partnership of 27 shares — one for each wife…"

The spoof was goofy enough to capture your attention and straight enough to make you wonder…briefly. However, an astonishing number of pretty sophisticated people gobbled it up. We got calls from all over: "Is the Sheikh on the level?"

One local social-climbing type beseeched us to let her have a cocktail party for him the next time he came to town. We were having so much fun with it that we decided to perpetuate it, milk it for all it was worth.

We then hired a very large, exceedingly bosomy, petulant-looking young woman and made her the number one wife, "Alydarlene." We dressed farm exercise riders, grooms, office staff, and maintenance workers — women and men (we were short-handed) — in harem outfits. They were heavily veiled, naturally, and they were cast as the other twenty-six wives who accompanied the sheikh on a heavily photographed subsequent visit.

Bin Had and Alydarlene arrived in the limousine, while the run-of-the-mill wives came in an old school bus that had been gutted for the storage of hay (After all, we were *not* Metro-Goldwyn-Mayer!).

Different sheikh-like scenarios were played out for three or four years, with Bin Had making more money from "modeling" than from hustling tips at the Hilton.

When Dogwood Stable hit the one-million-dollar mark for the first year, in 1983, we threw a big dance at the Piedmont Driving Club in Atlanta. An honored guest, of course, was the sheikh.

When my daughter Lila got married, her reception was held there, and, unbeknownst to her, Anne and I invited Sheikh Bin Had (in costume). When he entered the ballroom, just as the featured couple was having their wedding dance, it was like Moses parting the Red Sea. The guests did not know how to handle the sheikh.

I ushered him up to the dancing couple, and he cut in, briefly. The bride was delighted — about the dance, and the brevity of it.

We may bring Sheikh Bin Had out of retirement, but we'll wait for the hostilities in the Middle East to cool off! In the meantime, we've gotten our money's worth!

Good Old Fred and Jan Verzal

During Dogwood's existence, we have probably brought close to one thousand people into racing. Some stayed with us a long time; some left early. And I'm proud that we've been involved with some of the most important names in racing.

My present Dogwood roster of clients is Grade Triple A. But

in the formative years of my unorthodox career in racing, I was not as picky as I could afford to become later.

A fine example of "un-pickiness" I remember in particular was a large, loud-mouthed man named Fred. He lived in Atlanta, was a regional sales representative for a network of industrial magazines, and was a pretty good guy when he was sober, which was not often enough.

I had bought a two-year-old filly at the Hialeah sale in 1974. Her name was Jan Verzal. She looked and acted fast as hell, and Fred became one of five in the Dogwood partnership that would campaign her.

She broke her maiden first time out at Keeneland that April, and we then sent her up to River Downs in Cincinnati to run in the Breeze-a-Lea Stakes. Our boy Fred came up to "the River" to see the filly run, and, as usual, he arrived on the scene about "three sheets to the wind." He was one of those sloppy drunks who liked to get right in your face when you conversed. He liked to bet, and he had been plaguing me for days about whether, and even how much, he should bet (not my favorite topic!) on our filly.

When race time neared and the fillies were brought into the paddock, Freddy boy became more insistent, and his voice level jumped a few decibels. Jan had been saddled and was being walked around the ring.

"Well, shit! Should I bet on her or not?" Fred bellowed.

I could stand it no longer. With a worried look on my face, I said, "Well, Fred, I don't know what to tell you. The filly's been doing fine since her win at Keeneland. The only thing is, she has had a headache all morning, and she's been throwing up constantly since breakfast. Other than that, all systems are go!"

That did it. Fred groaned, threw up his hands, and made straight for the nearest bar. He didn't know any better.

She won easily.

Jan was fast, and now she'd won two. Undefeated! It was

mid-May, and we were gunning for bigger fields to conquer. We might have the best two-year-old filly in America!

The Fashion Stakes at Belmont Park in June was the next logical fixture, so we planned to send Jan Verzal to the Big Apple.

As the date got closer, I smoked out the race and talked with trainer Bob Dunham about the small field that was shaping up. The only horse of note was a filly trained by Frank Whiteley. She had been impressive in winning her maiden race by fifteen lengths. But, hell, we had won a stakes race; we had no fear of a horse that had just won a maiden race!

Dogwood was represented by a fairly large contingent, and, of course, good old Fred would not have passed up a festive opportunity of this sort. Actually, he was relatively subdued by the majesty of Belmont Park, and for this I was thankful. I didn't particularly want us to come across as a bunch of clowns in front of the New Yorkers.

Jan was second favorite in the race. Oddly enough, the filly that had just broken her maiden was the favorite. Now, how do you figure that? But, just wait. When they sprang the latch, old Jan would jerk a knot in that big hussy!

They broke, and Jan left there running! She could explode from the gate, and she did at the start of the five-furlong race, opening up three lengths in the first quarter. Lord have mercy! Looka here! We might as well head on down to the winner's circle. They'll never catch us today.

Jan moved toward the quarter pole. Then, Tommy Wallis, our rider, looked over his right shoulder and almost had a heart attack. A jet-black "typhoon" was about to envelop him and Jan Verzal. This monster blasted alongside and then did not get out of an open gallop as she cruised to the lead. She went on to crush us by nearly twenty lengths. We staggered home third.

What became of the filly that won the race? Her name was Ruffian. She had a fairly decent racing career.

What became of Fred? His conduct went from bad to worse, and I was able to buy him out of his ownership in our filly. I was also forced to insist that he not put a foot on Dogwood Farm property until he straightened himself out.

He didn't, and he never did.

Louie

One partner I will always remember, because he let me breathe a much-needed sigh of relief at a very crucial time in my horse career.

The man is Louie Roussel, a successful owner-trainer from New Orleans who won the Preakness and Belmont with Risen Star. He will have no recollection of that moment and what he did for me.

In the late eighties Dogwood had sold its farm in west central Georgia, closed its Atlanta office, and moved everything and everybody to Aiken, South Carolina. Concurrent with that unsettled time, we had bought some very expensive yearlings at the Keeneland July sale. We had placed them all into a very ambitious, high-priced package. Six horses, forty shares at $55,000 per share — $2,200,000 to raise. This was a big undertaking. If it didn't work, the ramifications would be disastrous.

We photographed the horses and printed elaborate brochures, mailing them out in late August to everyone we thought might be interested. This included a lot of professional horse people because we were offering such sire names as Nijinsky II, Northern Dancer, Danzig, and Raise a Native, for instance.

In early September I headed to Lexington again for the important fall sale. I did not have much heart for buying more stock because I already had a great deal on my plate, and I didn't know how fast I was going to be able to digest it. I was not exactly brimming over with confidence!

When I arrived at Keeneland, the barn area was teeming with horsemen looking over the yearlings for the sale two days

As a boy, the author was indelibly impressed by Man o' War and Will Harbut, the stallion's groom. The Phoenix Hotel in downtown Lexington once served as *the* place for deal-making and hobnobbing for everyone of import in the Thoroughbred industry.

The author's mother, Lila Campbell, saw Black Gold (pictured left after the 1924 Kentucky Derby) race for a final, heartbreaking time at Fair Grounds in New Orleans. The popular black colt was owned by Rosa Hoots (near left), an Osage Indian.

Everyone turns out for Aiken Trials (below), including the author, who is fifth from the right. Trainer John Gaver (below, inset) was a mainstay on the Aiken scene for many years and trained the Greentree Stable horses with an iron hand. Clayton O'Quinn (right) was an unforgettable character who called Ocala, Florida, home.

In its heyday, the Campbell family's Shoestring Farm was a force on the show horse scene and its young heir a rotund but able competitor.

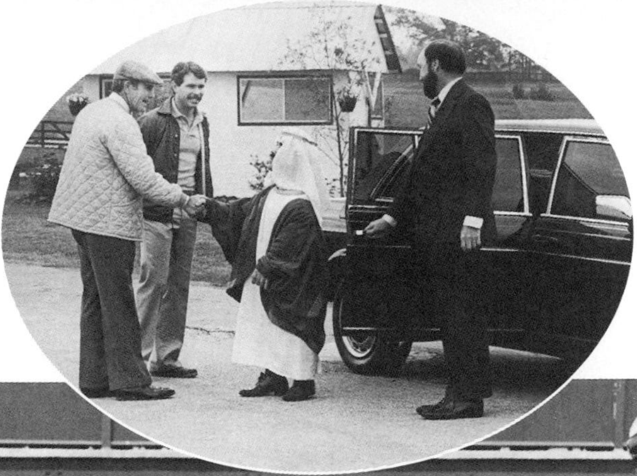

One of Dogwood Stable's first good runners, Jan Verzal (above in the Keeneland winner's circle) had the distinction of running behind the great filly Ruffian. Dogwood got a lot of mileage out of its pseudo-Sheikh Bin Had (top), who was actually a bellman in an Atlanta hotel. LeRoy Neiman, who sketched at a Derby post-position draw, failed to make an impression on one of his subjects, Sally Brown.

Cinzano (pictured right with Randy Rouse, who owned Cinzan
later in the horse's life) was a ringer in a peculiar betting scam.
match race between the Quarter Horse Stella Moore and Olymp
(on rail) resulted in a windfall for Olympia's owner, Fred Hoope

Two horses that made quite an impression were Kelso, shown with his two stable dogs, and the great trotter Greyhound, whom the author saw race against the clock at a Midwest fairgrounds.

hence. I knew I would encounter plenty of men and women who had received my offering. Would they have any interest in it? I was in bad need of, at least, winning a battle, if not necessarily the war. I wanted a sign that things were going to be okay.

I started down the horse path leading from the pavilion to the sales barns, catalog in hand, bravely setting out to look at new yearlings to purchase for money I was not sure I would have.

I will never forget approaching the first barn, in which the prime Spendthrift consignment had been situated for many years. Yearlings were being shown, and on this Saturday afternoon you couldn't have stirred the prospective buyers with a stick. I wondered if any of them had even considered my proposition. It sure seemed doubtful.

At that point I encountered Roussel, feet planted apart, glasses well down on his nose, catalog cradled in his arms, and engrossed in the inspection of a sharp-looking chestnut colt. His vet and several others were in his entourage.

Just as I walked by this group, Louie happened to glance up and see me. I nodded. He stared at me for about three seconds. You could see the wheels turning. Then, his voice dripping with New Orleans, he muttered as he resumed his inspection of the yearling:

"Ah'm in."

I knew what he meant. And right then I knew I was "home and dry." I was glad when he became a partner; but I was really ecstatic when I learned he was going to *become* one!

Now my "blood was up." There were thirty-nine more shares to sell, but the first sale made me confident the partnership would fill up. And it did, relatively easily.

Sally and LeRoy

Dogwood ran a horse named Jack Flash in the 1997 Kentucky Derby, and one of his partners was a delightful

Louisville lady named Sally Brown. Or Mrs. W.L. Lyons Brown.

Sally is a tiny lady, and she would not find me ungallant if I said she has a little age on her. She's a great character, very popular, and has a fine, old-Louisville pedigree.

The Derby post positions are drawn on Wednesday afternoon before the Saturday race, and it is a big media event. The participants are seated in rows of chairs, in front of a big mock starting gate on which post-position numbers are affixed, as they are determined. It's colorful, interesting of course, but a pretty big "to do" over a pretty simple exercise. Still, it's something you *must* do, if you've got a horse in the race.

Jack Flash had four connections at the draw. There were the trainer, Nick Zito, Sally Brown, Anne, and I. The other Dogwood partners had not yet arrived in town.

That year the official Derby artist was the renowned sports artist and horse racing fan, LeRoy Neiman, he of the Salvador Dali mustache. The dashing LeRoy had done an exciting, dramatic rendering of a Derby finish, and this was the visual theme of that year's Derby celebration.

The Jack Flash contingent was seated in a line on the second row, surrounded by other Derby-runners' connections. The media were situated in seats around the perimeter of the main assembly area within the Kentucky Derby Museum.

The proceedings, in the capable hands of Chris Lincoln, Dave Johnson, Tom Meeker, and other Churchill and ESPN dignitaries, commenced. While the numbers were being drawn, in the most possible suspenseful manner, I noticed that Neiman, some twenty-five yards away, seemed quite interested in our quartet. He was working on his sketchpad and looking up regularly to study us.

I thought Sally, an amateur artist, would get a kick out of the fact that the great LeRoy Neiman was sketching our picture. I tapped her on the arm and pointed over at Neiman. She understood what was happening. She looked over at him a few times, then opened her pocketbook and withdrew paper and a pen.

Now Neiman was sketching us, while Sally Brown was drawing him drawing us.

LeRoy Neiman had figured out what was happening, and he found it delightful that this cute little lady was so engaged.

In all of this we secured a post position (and where it was could not have mattered less since Jack Flash would drop back to last and then come with his run at the half-mile pole), and the affair drew to a close.

While we milled about, Neiman strode across the room, came up to us, ripped his sketch from his book and, with a flourish, presented it to Sally.

With a continental bow, and a charming smile, he said, "Now, may I have your sketch?"

With an indignant look on her face, Sally stared up at him. "No, you may not! Who are you anyway?"

He laughed and withdrew.

I told her moments later, "Sally, that man was LeRoy Neiman!"

"Never heard of him," she sniffed.

A Crashing Bore

While my own background has given me the utmost sympathy toward recovering alcoholics, that doesn't mean, by a long shot, that I revel in fraternizing with practicing alcoholics.

I am anxious to help those who want help. But until they reach that point, I want to stay clear of them. Nothing is more tiresome to an ex-drunk than a drunk!

And I have a flair for disengaging myself — from drunks or crashing bores. One night in Lexington, I demonstrated this technique, but not smoothly, I fear.

We were in Kentucky for the races, and so was a very nice

man from Alabama who owned part of a filly running in a stake. The man and wife, their son and daughter, and the wife's parents were joining Anne and me for dinner the night before.

We all met at 7:30. As we exchanged greetings, it did not take Sherlock Holmes to ascertain that the father-in-law was already feeling no pain. "Now let me warn you," my client told me, "Dad really knows his stuff when it comes to horseflesh." This turned out to be an accurate statement if one could only substitute a certain four-letter word for "flesh."

With only eight in the party, I could not manage to distance myself from "Dad" to the extent I desired, but I was able to seem heavily engaged with other tablemates whenever the father-in-law directed a conversational salvo my way.

But I'm good! You have never seen a man more enthusiastically engrossed in more distant conversations. When I heard "Dad" bleating, 'Say, Campbell, what the hell are you riding Don Brumfield for when Pat Day's in town?' I found refuge in interrogating his grandson about his summer camp activities.

When "Dad" could not get my attention, he turned to Anne, who is much more willing to suffer through the most excruciatingly boring conversational onslaught. After several more determined, but unsuccessful ventures to talk "horseflesh" with me, he zeroed in on Anne as a much more gratifying target.

However, he hadn't entirely forgotten me. I could see him glare disgustedly down the table from time to time.

At the end of the evening, he leaned toward his wife, jerked a thumb in my direction, and announced, "That son of a bitch doesn't know what he's talking about anyway. His wife's the only one knows what's going on!"

5

Bookmakers

I'm sure it's a wondrously efficient world that permits us to sit in a simulcasting center at a racetrack or in an off-track betting parlor and bet every five minutes or so on a different horse (and maybe even a dog!) in a different town. It wears me out to think about it.

August Belmont would turn over in his grave. But if this is what it takes to make our sport viable, then I'm all for it. Even the addition of slot machines.

Through the years my betting patterns have changed in direct proportion to my involvement in the sport and business of racing horses.

When I was simply an avid fan, with trips to the track on a frustratingly infrequent basis, I would probably have had a heart attack if I had arrived too late to play the daily double. Leave before the last race? Are you crazy?

I adored betting on horses.

But when I got into the horse business around thirty-five years ago, the campaigning of horses began to quench my thirst for gambling. I'd rather watch the post parade than stand in line at the windows.

I still like making a bet, but only in the odd circumstance where I feel — usually mistakenly — that I'm orchestrating a betting coup that permits me to take an edge. Those are times when Jupiter aligns with Mars in the equine heavens, when the horse is in an easy spot and no one knows it but me.

I have not exactly broken up the game with these "killings," but I sure have had fun trying, including those failures that severely damaged my pocketbook.

These endeavors, by their nature, usually have involved a bookmaker, and that has always heightened the titillation.

While I generally do not applaud lawbreakers, I must admit: I do like bookmakers. In the first place, practically all of them are impeccably honest. They have to be, or they wouldn't be in business. A gambler lives and dies by his word.

There was a period while I lived in Atlanta during which "Sheriff," the local bookie, found it prudent to declare a moratorium on his operations due to increased scrutiny by law enforcement.

In those days I enjoyed making a few bets on major stakes races on Saturdays.

It was not difficult to instead contact a bookmaker in Louisville. His name was Barney (a suitable name for one who plied that trade, I felt). Barney supplied me with his mailing address; he did not wish to do business by telephone, as he was quite squeamish about the gendarmes tapping his phone and learning he was gambling across state lines. Louisville police certainly understood the logic of betting on horses within the confines of their city, but commerce of a regional nature violated their sensibilities.

My custom was to figure out bets for the upcoming Saturday and then on Tuesday or Wednesday mail to Barney an epistle containing my selections along with the legal tender to support them. Periodically, he would remit to me, if there were a need. And there usually wasn't!

One week I fancied the fine router Hill Rise to win the San Juan Capistrano at Santa Anita. I mailed this info, along with a double sawbuck, to Barney. When the race was run on Saturday afternoon, Hill Rise was not victorious. So I lost the twenty, a fairly significant amount to me, but not ruinous by any means.

The following Wednesday I received a letter in the mail from good old Barney. It read, "I am returning your money. Your letter did not arrive in time."

Extraordinary! Who knew this but Barney? Talk about honesty!

Doing Business with Sheriff

The aforementioned Sheriff operated for many years in Atlanta. Sheriff dealt primarily in football in that non-racing town, but he understood and booked bets on horse racing, as long as it was a major track. If you wanted to bet some bush track like Miles Park or Sunshine Park or River Downs, your action was not for Sheriff.

This Atlanta bookmaker, like all others at that time, had a universal set of regulations concerning payoffs. No matter what the horse paid at the track, you got a max of 15-1 on a win, 6-1 on place, and 3-1 on show. Sheriff did not seem to have access to good horse racing lay-off connections, where, for instance, he could call Cincinnati or Cleveland, and parcel out ("lay-off") a portion of the action on a certain horse, in case he felt that it was dangerously excessive. If you wanted to bet more than fifty dollars on one horse, Sheriff got nervous and said "no dice."

I never actually met Sheriff. My code name was "C.C." I had his telephone number. He did not have mine. We settled up the next day, and through the years, this was done at various places.

The first was a shop where men's hats were cleaned and blocked. You simply came in, looked somewhat deliberately into the eyes of the old Greek proprietor, uttered your code name and, wordlessly, he shoved a small envelope in your hands. Conversely, if things had not gone your way, you made sure no hat customers were watching the transaction and then offered your envelope to him.

Sheriff liked to receive envelopes the very next day.

Either the hat shop or Sheriff saw fit to terminate the drop point, so for several years we did business at a variety of newsstands, always run by Greek gentlemen. I assumed Sheriff himself was of that national origin.

His voice was quite distinctive. You remember Marlon Brando as The Godfather? That was the voice of Sheriff. Right out of Central Casting.

My father made the occasional bet with Sheriff and was known as "Shoestring." And I put others in touch with him.

I had one particular friend in Atlanta whose name was Ward Bordeau, and he was an obstetrician. He was an old New Orleans boy, knew the ways of the racetrack, and he liked to bet on horses. He wanted a connection for this purpose, so I put him together with "the man." And they did steady business.

Since Ward ("Doc" was his *nom de guerre*) was often up all night delivering babies, it followed that he was not as precisely punctual with his envelopes as Sheriff preferred.

Once when I called Sheriff to make a bet, he seemed a little grumpier than usual. Finally, he came out with it.

"Where in the hell's Doc? I ain't heard from him in a while. He owes me."

I said, "I don't know, Sheriff. I haven't seen him."

Then in a completely stupid, misguided effort at humor, which I should have known he would not have enjoyed, I said, "You know, Doc is an obstetrician. He delivers babies. Maybe if he doesn't pay you, he'll give you a little baby to play with! But you don't need a baby, do you Sheriff (HaHa)?"

Long silence. "I don't need no friggin' baby."

Lexington — the Mother Lode

Bookmakers are an endangered species. You rarely hear the term anymore. Legalized off-track betting operations have done them in. In the old days when they were known as handbooks, the Fayette County grand jury listed forty-six Lexington addresses that were identified as handbooks. According to Maryjean Wall, the fine Turf writer for the *Lexington Herald-Leader,* this number represented more than half of the total number of churches in the town!

Handbooks were all over Lexington in the thirties and forties, and they catered to different strata of clientele. Some would take bets for as little as ten cents or twenty-five cents; others, like the book at the Drake Hotel, tended to cater more to the "finger bowl" trade. There, a racing paper was furnished, drinks passed, and other amenities provided for the players, many of whom were professional horsemen.

Lexington is a horse town, and practically everyone, except the odd preacher, would have an occasional need to bet on a racehorse. Generally, the bookmakers were also pretty good citizens. They tended to play by the rules and keep their noses clean.

One important no-no was that when Keeneland was operating, the books were shut down. They did *not* compete with Keeneland.

These handbooks subscribed to the wire service controlled by a well-connected gentleman out of Cleveland named Mushy Wexler. Wire service communications started with a man in the grandstand at Belmont, Hialeah, Pimlico, etc., who would signal the results by a variety of means to an associate in a nearby location. That fellow, a telegrapher, would quickly "move" the results to Cleveland and then on to the subscribers: the handbooks in Lexington, New Orleans, or wherever.

Sometimes, the deluxe bookie establishments would actually re-create the running of the race for the pleasure or displeasure of customers in the room. If you saw the movie *The Sting,* you've got the picture.

Huntington

I miss the books. It's like a lot of things today: too much technology, not enough individual...for me. Some of the romance is gone from betting on horses.

Huntington, West Virginia, was a sporty little town when I lived there in 1950.

Bookmakers have always found poolrooms compatible places in which to headquarter, and a major bookie in Huntington, named Billy Miles, operated out of the huge Monarch Grill. This establishment offered pool and billiards, bar service, and wonderfully indigestible sandwiches like Limburger cheese and tongue, liverwurst and onions, and Polish sausage. In addition to these amenities, old Billy strolled amiably around the tables, at your service for almost any kind of action. And, due to its proximity to Kentucky, there was keen interest in the horses at Keeneland and Churchill Downs.

Billy never seemed to sit down. He just rambled in and out of the tables, his pockets bulging with notes, entries, and currency, until he stopped for a whispered conference with a shooter or customer who simply came in to "do business" with Billy.

Calumet — in that era and every other — had a stable full of good horses. One I loved dearly was Hill Gail, and I bet him and most other horses carrying the devil's red and blue colors almost automatically. One day I went into the Monarch and spotted Billy as he dodged around the action of a snooker table. I walked up and got right to the point. I said, "Hi, Billy, Hill Gail in the Derby Trial." I then offered my two dollars in a very straightforward manner. I thought he'd have a stroke.

He hissed, "Goddamn, man! Don't hand me no money like that. No telling who's in here watching us!"

When you did engage Billy in the manner he preferred, you might as well have put a banner over your heads saying, "we're doing something we should not be doing."

He had a little number he liked to do. Billy would go into sort of a crouch, and then with his eyes darting surreptitiously around the room, he was ready to receive the order. When money changed hands, he would push his stomach up against you as a shield, in a maneuver that looked as if you were preparing to dance. Then, with his arms stiffly by his sides, his fingers crept into action and did the job of removing the money from your hands to his pockets. All this theatrical "shtick" was accompanied by a sudden serene expression on Billy's countenance meant to convey childlike innocence and nonchalance.

Billy liked making book, but he also liked playing the role of a bookmaker.

"Britches" of Nashville

My father used to bet with a bookmaker in Nashville by the name of "Britches."

I sometimes went along with my dad to Britches' handbook on Church Street to do business. It was ostensibly an establishment where one would go to buy a magazine or newspaper. However, these items were in ridiculously short supply. In the corner of the room, a magazine rack displayed a discouraged-looking assortment of month-old publications. You could have found more current reading matter in the waiting room of a struggling chiropractor.

The focal point of the room was a large counter, behind which an anemic-looking staffer was usually smoking a cigar. But the cunning touch of the entire operation was that arrayed on this counter were perhaps five magazines, of fairly recent vintage.

There might be a *Photoplay, Silver Screen, Look, Life,* and, with a salute to distaff customers, a *Ladies' Home Journal.*

The contents of each had been gutted. In one would be today's entries from Pimlico; in the second there would be Arlington Park. *Ladies' Home Journal* might offer the selections for a wager at Hollywood Park. And so on.

Should an accomplished sleuth from a concerned law enforcement agency have come in seeking evildoers, the true nature of Britches' commercial operation might have been revealed.

That never happened. A gentler, more civilized time?

Clockers

A vital link in the relationship between the gambler and the institution (formal or informal) receiving the gamble is the clocker, artisans about whom an entire book could be justified.

Clockers are born, not made. Imagine: with one hundred horses on the racetrack at peak periods, these men must observe, identify, time, and remember every horse that is breezing. They are not inclined toward sociability, but neither do they seem to be frenzied. Perched high in the grandstand in an empty box, in extreme cold or scorching heat, the clocker has about thirty seconds from the time the horse leaves the quarter pole until it goes around the clubhouse turn. This is the crucial portion of the "work." All the clocker has to do is to split the fractions (most trainers want to know the time of the final quarter or eighth), observe the markings or saddle cloth to help identify the critter, decide how easily the horse galloped out...and record it all.

Not many human beings possess the equanimity to handle this job.

This goes on every morning from daylight (and often before!) until about ten o'clock. It is a high-pressure job akin to being an air controller.

In one of the great tales of the Turf, Colonel Phil Chinn is supposed to have dug up and rearranged the location of the quarter pole so as to record a "blistering" workout for an inferior animal that was for sale and needed all the help he could get.

In the old days, though, the trainer or owner with a gambling bent quickly realized it might be easier to move the clocker than the poles. So times being hard and human nature being what it is, alliances and deals were sometimes made that put the clocking game under a suspicious cloud.

In the last thirty years new racing states have been added. Consequently, there are many new racetracks; thus more jobs today for clockers. In the old days, clocking jobs were scarce as hen's teeth. Those so employed had to rely on creativity and razor sharpness to survive.

Clockers have had great Runyonesque names like Smokey, The Earl, Longboy, Bundleboy, the Librarian, and Holdout Sam. One of the sharpest and most erudite, and a great favorite of mine, is a colorful fellow who clocked for many years in Florida. This would be Ted Tamer, now retired and leading the good life in South Carolina.

Indian Charlie (the Original)

Perhaps the most famous clocker of our day was Indian Charlie, not to be confused with today's gossip sheet writer who has borrowed "Indian Charlie" as a *nom de plume.* The original was a highly intelligent, intellectual man, with more than a hint of mystery about him and a character of enormous respect. Just as the Indians seemed to have a supernatural faculty for knowing unknowable things, so did Indian Charlie have that instinct about a racehorse.

I associate his perspicacity with two of our horses. One was one of the best racehorses of his day. The other was a $10,000 claimer. I dearly loved them both, and both were extremely important in my life.

Summer Squall was the first; Memphis Lou was the second.

When Squall came out of winter quarters as a two-year-old, he left Aiken with a big reputation. From the time I got this Storm Bird colt as a yearling, it was clear he had the ability to "scorch the earth" and was immensely interested in so doing!

He acted like something special from the time Ron Stevens, Dogwood's longtime farm trainer, started breaking him.

We ran him in the Aiken Trials, going a quarter mile, and he ran third in a four-horse field! When the break came in that explosive, short dash, Summer Squall was gazing out at the infield. The field left; then he left. He just failed to catch the winner, after spotting them all about one-sixteenth of a mile.

But he came out of South Carolina a week later with the light having been illuminated! I shipped him to Keeneland to run in one of those four-and-half-furlong baby races. Neil Howard was to train him. He got him, liked him, saw that he was ready to run, and put him in the entries. (He said he was "a baked cake — all I had to do was run him in the oven!")

Summer Squall romped home by eleven lengths on April 20, 1989. As I went jubilantly down to the winner's circle, I walked past Indian Charlie.

He gave me a sly grin, cocked his thumb toward the colt galloping back, and said, "That's the one you been waitin' on, Cot."

While clockers are practically all legit now and make good money doing what they are supposed to do, again we go back to the bad old, good old days, when these boys often needed to supplement incomes with other revenue-producing endeavors.

Touts

Some clockers drifted logically into an enterprise known as "touting." In case you don't know about this practice, which also is becoming a bona fide dinosaur today, a tout sells information about participants in a horse race. The buyers are keenly interested in germane facts vital to selecting a winner.

The clocker is employed by the racetrack to clock horses in the morning. He observes the fast ones and the slow ones. Is there, then, a more authoritative source of information about the capabilities of competing horses? Ostensibly not. So clocking and touting did tend to be vocations that complemented one another beautifully.

Some touts practiced the quality approach. They sought to handicap the race correctly and then convince a bettor, or bettors, that Wagonmaster would win the fifth, thus making them entitled to a percentage of the winning payoff if they were correct. If they proved to be flagrantly incorrect, they moved on to another area in the grandstand. If they came close, they stuck around to commiserate about the rotten racing luck that brought failure for what otherwise would have been a piece of cake.

Then there were touts that took the quantity approach. In a perfect world, in a ten-horse race they found ten customers and gave each a different horse. Afterward, one would be delighted while two or three others might not be fully disgusted with some juice left in the lemon. To hell with the rest of them. If you make an omelet, you've got to break some eggs.

Meeting Colonel Clay

Sometimes the tout was already acquainted with the mark; sometimes he depended on his ability to strike up a very fast friendship. And a rapidly approaching post time often worked in favor of the tout. Many touts worked in teams, and the thespian talents of some were magnificent indeed.

I remember so well being accosted by, and delighted with, a trio of touts some years ago at Churchill Downs on Derby week. This highly charged, super-festive event is happy hunting ground for all sorts of hustles. It is a goldmine for touts.

First, I was overdressed, looking like a tourist. I had on white pants, a blue blazer, white bucks, and nice white shirt and tie. I looked like I was going to a garden party. Sucker was written all over me.

It was Oaks Day, a Friday. A tremendous crowd was on hand, and I had just walked into the betting area and was taking a last look at my program before going to the window. When I glanced up, two pleasant-looking fellows were standing fairly close to me. They casually looked toward me, smiled, and spoke in an appealing, mellow manner that indicated we might be acquainted. They did seem vaguely familiar.

"Who do you like in this race? Pretty tough, huh?" one guy asked me.

"Well, I guess I would have to…" I started out.

Just then, one of the men interrupted, excitedly pointing toward the windows, "Oh, my God, here comes Colonel Clay. Let's see what he's doing. He knows; if he'll just tell us!"

At that point, a solid-looking older fellow sauntered up to our impromptu trio and paused distractedly while he shuffled through a significant stack of mutuel tickets.

"Howdy, Colonel, do you remember me? I'm Willis Sears," one them said, pumping the hand of the "Colonel," a clearly important man.

"Whadda ya think of this race?"

The Colonel smiled benevolently, shook his head disapprovingly as if he were speaking to foolish children, and said, "Now, boys, if you can't make up your own mind, you've got no business betting on racehorses." The strong, very convincing implication was that the Colonel did.

He now looked over at me and said, "How do you do, sir. I'm Lawrence Clay. You're not with these bad boys are you?"

"Colonel, I haven't cashed a ticket all day! Who do you like in this race?" pleaded one of my new "friends."

The Colonel was now rifling through his tickets again, and his attention shifted to the tote board, which showed two minutes to post time.

Again, the other confederate joined in the entreaty for betting information. "Man, talk to us! We're going to be shut out at the windows. Those lines are long." Now it was a foregone conclusion: the Colonel definitely did know which horse was going to win this race, and the secret to a successful stay in Louisville for us three was literally on the lips of this insider.

The Colonel gave in, chuckling indulgently. "All right! All right! You'll never get your bet down now. I'll let you have one of my tickets. Give me a hundred."

Both fellows thrust a bill at the Colonel, and he handed each one of his tickets. He then turned toward me, as if it were a foregone conclusion that he was going to have to include me in this aggravating obligation to save the day for three idiots.

"Come on, let's go! I've got to get back to my guests in the box. You can get one of my tickets, but we're running out of time!"

At that point the scam dawned on me. I smiled in appreciation, said no thanks, and walked away.

Moments later I looked back. The Colonel had gone over by the windows; the other two partners were moving over toward another mark. There was just barely enough time for them to try it again.

What a performance! They didn't get it, but they really deserved my hundred dollars. By the way, my money would have bought a non-winning one-hundred-dollar ticket from yesterday or the day before…picked up off the floor by "stoopers," and sold cheaply to the Colonel and his men as props to ensnare bigger game.

6

Betting Coups

Indian Charlie, the legendary clocker, called the shot correctly when he prophesied Summer Squall's greatness. Much earlier he had commented unerringly on a horse of only momentary celebrity. His name was Memphis Lou, and he was the epitome of the storied gallantry of the Thoroughbred.

I bought Memphis Lou out of a mud pit backyard from an old man in Georgetown, Kentucky. A big, fat slob of an unbroken two-year-old, Memphis Lou developed into a sleek black horse with a heart of pure hickory.

God gave Memphis only limited ability but endowed him with an indomitable, workmanlike spirit. What a human being he would have been!

He campaigned as a solid $10,000 claimer in the early seventies. We adored him, and luckily he was never claimed from Dogwood. We were careful not to let him drop into a claiming neighborhood in which he would be irresistibly tempting. On the other hand, if we raised him much above $10,000, he would get beat, but through no lack of trying.

Midway in his life with Dogwood, a paralyzed vocal chord caused wind problems. He underwent surgery to correct this, and then we turned him out on the farm for six months.

When the old boy returned, he was as good as ever.

Because he had thrown in a couple of inferior races when

his breathing was not good, because of his hiatus from competition, because he was getting sharp as hell, and because you could stake your life on him when he was right — here was a lovely betting opportunity!

I have always appreciated this sort of "special" wagering situation.

We got old Memphis ready right on the farm, and then we shipped him to Churchill Downs. We worked him once there, before the sun was up, and he sizzled five furlongs in :59 flat.

Memphis Lou was as sharp as jailhouse coffee.

We still needed an "edge," so we entered him in a $3,500 claiming race. On paper this horse did not look good. Were we trying to get rid of a crippled horse, stuff him down someone's throat? The typical crafty claiming trainer was going to watch him run once before taking him.

Training this horse for Dogwood was the ideal man for a bet-cashing project of this sort. Bill Gateman understood, appreciated, and intended to participate in this delicious caper. He was like a sphinx about such matters. And he had suggested the ideal jockey: Weston J. "Buddy" Soirez, hardly a household name but a good, capable rider.

Now Memphis was put in the entries. He got in the fifth race at Churchill, $3,500 claimers going six furlongs, and, by design, the day of the week was Saturday, a heavy crowd day at the storied Louisville track.

We bet money with the bookmakers in New Orleans, Atlanta, St. Louis, and Pawtucket, Rhode Island. We then flew to Louisville to lay more through the windows. Fortunately, Dogwood also had a horse in the stake at Churchill that day to explain the presence of our little group at the racetrack.

We went to the windows in shifts, keeping a close eye on the fluctuating odds. Thankfully, there was a "sure thing" in the race, a 4-5 shot that was dropping down from an easy win at five thousand dollars. That Memphis was going to the post with all the verve of an old milk cow, his customary pre-race demeanor, did not cause a stampede to the windows. There was really just no reason for anyone but us to bet on him!

Memphis Lou opened at 5-1, at one point shortened to 5-2, but then drifted up to close at 7-2, a price we were glad to settle for.

Post time.

The starter sprang the latch, and the field started down the backstretch. Memphis Lou was laying fourth, about four lengths off the lead, and Soirez had a "half-nelson" on the old boy.

Looks like this gun is loaded; all we gotta do is pull the trigger!

Through the turn they proceeded in that manner. When they hit the quarter pole, Soirez wheeled Memphis out for the drive and had a clear path ahead. At the three-sixteenths pole, he clucked twice, shook the reins at him, and it was "Good-bye, baby, so long!"

Memphis Lou took off like a scalded dog, collared the favorite at the sixteenth pole, and went past him like he was tied to a tree. Our horse won by four lengths, "as the rider pleased."

How very sweet it was! He paid $9.40. It was the right move, with the right horse, on the right day.

After the race and the boisterous winner's circle ceremonies, we went back to a TV monitor in the clubhouse to watch the replay.

At that point I looked over at a grinning Indian Charlie standing nearby. The wily clocker looked at me, shook his head, and said, "That's the greatest robbery since the days of Jesse James!"

Absolutely nothing is more fun than trying to mastermind a score of that sort. I'd hate to do it for a living and would starve in the process. But to take a shot every couple of years or so is delicious. Even if you don't win.

Garden Gate (Or "The Anatomy of a Failure")

I doubt my name will ever be grouped among such legendary racetrack plungers as Pittsburgh Phil, Lucky Baldwin, Art Rooney, Arnold Rothstein, and Bet-a-Million Gates. But I am a few inches closer, thanks to an educational gambling venture involving a modestly bred filly named Garden Gate. This venture came to fruition at Thistledown Race Track in Cleveland.

Garden Gate was a three-year-old filly possessing big speed. Cheap speed, admittedly. She trained terrifically on the farm, and I decided she should be the vehicle that, properly managed, could have us all wearing diamonds.

I decided for some strange reason that Cleveland, Ohio, was the very spot for her racing debut — and the opportunity for a very important betting triumph.

A venture of this sort requires the proper trainer, and I had just the adventurous type. His name was Grover Hull. And Grover licked his chops when first I outlined my intentions with Garden Gate.

This would be a piece of cake, as long as I sent him a horse that could *run* a little bit!

I shipped the filly up to Grover. About a week after she got to Thistledown, I flew up so Grover and I could watch her work together. Well, she did convince Grover she could run. So I left town happy with the arrangements.

Grover's appearance and personality were interesting. First, he measured out about six-foot-six, tipped the scales at around 250, and sweated a lot. He had an intriguing tonsorial treatment — exceedingly long hair swept aft on the sides, but crew-cut flat on top. Further, he was never seen, day or night, without what seemed to be jet-black glasses, with frames the size of demitasse saucers. Grover was by no means inconspicuous.

When I left Cleveland, Grover and I had worked out a

timetable that called for "G-Day," our secret campaign code name, to take place in about a month. Every minute detail had to be worked out and massaged to exquisite perfection.

Grover and I conferred on the phone nightly, and the reports from his end were glowing. His main objective was not to tip our mitt and let the world know we had a race filly of extraordinary ability. She must be kept under wraps! Grover didn't want his help to know about her speed, so that when she did work, she was rarely permitted more than an open gallop.

Our phone conversations were very reassuring. The only discordant note was that Mrs. Hull, who invariably answered the phone (Grover seemed to be "resting" much of the time at home), did not seem to care for me. In fact, she seemed to like Grover even less!

I can hear her cheery greeting now. After several rings, this disgusted voice would be heard: "Awright!" This signaled the caller to state his business (and be damned quick about it).

"Mrs. Hull, this is Cot Campbell. How are *you*? I wonder if I might speak to Grover, please ma'am?" This, I am afraid, was delivered in a disgustingly unctuous manner, for I strove to preserve Grover's domestic tranquility for the overall good of "The Plan."

Upon hearing this jovial salutation, Mrs. Hull would respond by slamming down the instrument and bellowing, "It's fer *yew*, Grover!"

Grover and I discussed the well-being of Garden Gate, of course. We also covered such details as who would ride her and how to curry favor with the racing secretary so if the upcoming condition book had no suitable race, he would "put up" an extra and then strive to make it fill. We needed to school the filly in the gate and make sure the gate crew assigned the right man to her head and that the starter would not push the button until he was sure our filly was poised for action.

The new condition book came out, and, sure enough,

included in it was precisely the race Grover had requested for us: maiden, claiming ($2,500). Three-year-old fillies going six furlongs. It would go, the secretary promised him. The date was May 19, ten days away.

That night on the phone, Grover and I went down the checklist. Rider? Danny Weiler, perennial leading rider at Thistledown. Gate crew? The boys knew the filly, and she had gotten her gate card. Broke like a shot! The perfect race was awaiting us. Grooms? Clockers? Nobody knew anything. What could go wrong?

On the eve of the race, I flew to Cleveland, accompanied by my aforementioned party-boy partner Albert Warner. I had withdrawn $6,600 to bet on the filly. Albert had his own funds, and Grover was certainly planning to back her.

Garden Gate was in the first race, number nine in a field of nine fillies.

I had been unable to find any bookmakers willing to accept wagers on this small track, so all the money was to be wagered on track, although we did have a tenuous connection with a Cleveland handbook, and we had reason to think we could lay off some of it with him. His name was Mushy Wexler, mentioned earlier as head of the wire service that supplied data to bookmakers. A mutual connection in Atlanta had suggested this source for part of our wagers and had supposedly called Mushy for us. We were set to transact our business at Mushy's restaurant in downtown Cleveland, the Theatrical Grill.

When we hit town, I made a hurried call to Grover (the first of five or six before the next afternoon). We agreed that Albert, Grover, and I would dine at the Theatrical Grill, while doing business with Mr. Wexler.

I'm sure our trio looked like men on a serious mission to Mushy when he arrived several hours into the meal. I do not think our project ranked very high on his priority list. But he sat with us for a few minutes in our banquette and agreed to "handle" two thousand dollars for us. He did point out that Thistledown, with its very small handle, was an exceptionally stupid selection for such a venture. "Hell, if you bet a lousy five hundred dollars through the windows, she'll go off at 2-5!"

He had a good point, one I should have thought of several months earlier.

The next morning I went early to Grover's barn, so I could stare at the filly for a while. Then I went back to the hotel to prepare for the festivities. Thankfully, Garden Gate was in the first race, so there weren't too many agonizing hours to while away.

Albert and I, without prior consultation, had decided to put on our glad rags. This was not smart; covertness should have been our watchword. Thistledown is not known for its sartorial splendor, so the clientele knew we were there "for the reason and not for the season." Clearly something important had lured us.

First post was one o'clock. After we had choked down a hot dog around noon — Albert managing a bourbon or two to wash his down — the windows opened so we could commence wagering.

Number Nine (Garden Gate) opened at 10-1. In the first ninety-second flash on the tote board, she dropped to 8-5. What the hell! We hadn't even made our first bet! Whose money? Mushy Wexler? Grover? Is the big secret out all over Cleveland?

I bet one thousand dollars, and she dropped to 1-9. Not 9-1, mind you.

I saw that it would be counter-productive to continue to bet her, so I decided to begin wheeling her in the daily double. I stood at the window for fifteen minutes and kept betting Number Nine in the first race with every horse in the second race. I bet another one thousand dollars in this manner. Albert, very considerately in view of the situation, said he would refrain from betting anything.

At 12:35 the horses came into the paddock to be saddled for the first race. When Garden Gate hove into distant view, she looked like "sunrise in the paint factory." Good Lord! Grover had braided her mane, forelock, and tail in festive green and yellow. The groom and hot walker were adorned in homemade green and yellow coordinates. We might as well have had banners made and brought along some cheerleaders. The short price on the tote board, of course, further attested to our aspirations for Garden Gate.

Grover, lumbering along with the filly, had chosen for the day a quiet ensemble: a stark white, slightly modified zoot suit, black shirt with red accessories.

There were no more than seventy-five human beings around the paddock for the first race, but 150 eyes had to be glued to the colorful connections of Number Nine.

The filly behaved quite well during the saddling (steady schooling had been part of the plan, you will remember). The rider, Danny Weiler, strode over to our group. There was a good bit of head nodding, smirking, winking, and knowing looks as Grover articulated the simple strategy for the race: break and go. Albert insisted on making about ten photographs (just in case someone on the premises had failed to notice our little entourage). The racing secretary even came in to "pay his respects."

The horses left the paddock for the post parade. Grover, sweating heavily now, and Albert went to a position at the finish line, while I descended into the bowels of Thistledown and bet one thousand dollars to win and another to place. Why not? At this point it was the successful completion of the exercise, not the monetary reward, that mattered. I scurried up to the appointed meeting place and fell in with my two accomplices.

The odds on Garden Gate were now 1-5.

It was the moment of truth. The first race was off!

Garden Gate "beat" the gate. Three jumps and she was on top by two lengths. They were going six furlongs, and by the time she had gone a quarter of a mile she was leading by six lengths! How sweet it was! I was screaming bloody murder, Albert was beating me on the back, and Grover kept murmuring, "I *knew* that bitch could run!"

Into the turn she went, maintaining that wonderful margin.

Now Weiler wheeled her into the stretch, and the glory and gold were only a quarter-mile away. Garden Gate now had a five-length lead, but there was a filly chasing her, and she was coming with a good run.

Grover screamed, "She's getting tired, but they'll never catch her today!"

"I don't know, Grover," I replied. That other filly was coming hard at the eighth pole, and our girl had only a three-length lead.

At the sixteenth pole Weiler was frantically showering down on Garden Gate, and her lead had dwindled to one length.

"Oh my God! Get there, baby. Come on wire!"

About six jumps from home, Garden Gate just about slowed to a walk, and I will never forget that sickening feeling as that other filly seemed to catapult past Garden Gate. She won the race by a widening length, and Garden Gate was a neck ahead of the third horse.

I looked at Grover. He was wringing wet. He mopped his brow, shook his head sagely, and said, "She ran well. She needed the race. Man, they'll pay hell beating this hussy the next time!"

The filly had schooled in the gate and the paddock, the racing secretary was in our corner and had written precisely the race we wanted, the gate crew had seen to it that she got a clean break, the filly had received painstaking care. There was only one other matter that was left unattended.

Grover had not gotten around to training her to run six furlongs. She was fit enough for five…but not six.

The plane trip back to Atlanta was a long one.

She won her next start (maiden special weight) by ten lengths. But the big train had already run…and been derailed.

Olympia

In the case of the celebrated horseman Fred Hooper, his legendary bet on Olympia in 1949 was not a betting coup per se. It was just sheer, unadulterated guts, a commodity of which this great horseman had more than his share.

The lanky Alabaman had scuffled and hustled all his life, and he was no stranger to risk. Hooper got his start by enrolling in the Moler Barber College in Atlanta. After he had completed the curriculum — in a couple of days — he packed his comb, scissors, and clippers and headed for the big construction camps that were mushrooming across Dixie. He cut hair. While so engaged, the basic rudiments of the construction game rubbed off on him.

Soon he began bidding on inconsequential jobs. It wasn't much longer before Hooper Construction Company was paving highways and building airports. It became one of the South's largest construction companies.

This farm boy had always had an interest in horses and understood horse racing. In 1943 he indulged himself. He went to the Keeneland sale and bought a yearling by Sir Gallahad III. He named him Hoop, Jr. for his son, and two years later Fred won the Kentucky Derby with his very first horse.

He tried the Derby with some of his other cracks — Admiral's Voyage, Crozier, and Olympia — but never won it again.

However, Olympia, ill-suited as he was for the mile and a quarter, turned out to be one of the fastest horses of all time and a predominant speed influence on the breed. It was

Olympia who was to represent the Thoroughbred in one of the shortest, and most dramatic, races ever run: the famous match race against the fastest Quarter Horse in the world.

Stella Moore was her name and a quarter-mile was her game!

Stella had defeated a very fast California Thoroughbred named Fair Truckle. The swift mare's owners next approached Hooper and threw down the gauntlet: quarter mile, Tropical Park in Miami, $25,000 put up by each side, Stella Moore versus Olympia.

The super-quick Olympia was as game as Dick Tracy. And so was Fred Hooper. Done!

There was to be no pari-mutuel wagering on this match race. It was an exhibition, approved by the state.

The race was on, and a sellout crowd filled the Tropical Park grandstand. Half the attendees showed up in ten-gallon hats and cowboy boots. And they were loaded with Stella Moore money.

Fred Hooper covered every dime of it and was looking for more at post time.

In charge of these special proceedings was the racing secretary of Tropical Park, Pat Farrell. A big part of his job that day was recording the bets. As he received money (legal tender), he pushed it into the top right drawer of his desk and locked it. At post time, he then locked the door to the racing secretary's office and rushed out to see the making of racing history.

At this point Hooper had put up his $25,000 stake, as had Stella's man, and Hooper had single-handedly covered about one hundred grand in bets from numerous Quarter Horse enthusiasts. This was very big money in the late forties.

When the starter sprung the latch, Olympia flashed his vaunted speed, got the drop on Stella Moore, and held her safe to the wire, winning by the rapidly vanishing margin of a head.

The finish was scary, but not nearly as scary as the settling of the bets.

After pictures were taken and hands were shaken, a big crowd went back to Pat Farrell's office for the settling-up ceremonies.

With a big smile on his face, Pat withdrew his key from his pocket, held it up as a magician might have, and with a flourish inserted it into the lock on the drawer. He flung the drawer open for one and all to behold the absolutely staggering cache of greenbacks, now belonging to Fred Hooper.

The drawer was empty.

Pat Farrell looked as if he would lose his lunch. His face was ashen, and he thrust his hand into the drawer as if he might be able to feel the money, even though he certainly could not see it!

The atmosphere in the room was decidedly tense.

Finally, Farrell jerked the drawer completely out of the desk. The bigger drawer beneath it was housing a truly splendid clump of greenbacks. There was the stash of cash.

There was no back panel in the top drawer, so as Farrell hurriedly pushed the final batch of bills toward the back of the drawer, the dough had dropped out of sight into the bottom compartment.

Hooper collected, gave a grand to Pat (slowly recovering from a near coronary!), nodded politely to the vanquished cowboys, and headed back to the barn. It had been a great day for the breed.

Cinzano and Lebon

Let us examine the anatomy of a blighted betting coup:

Cinzano was the best horse in Uruguay. Lebon couldn't outrun a fat man going uphill.

But they looked almost exactly alike.

Ahhh!

According to the records of a court trial, in which a famous veterinarian, Dr. Mark Gerard, was convicted of "fraudulent practice in a contest of speed," the good doctor went to South America and bought both animals (ostensibly for the ownership of one Jack Morgan, also subsequently registered as trainer of the animals).

What followed was one of the most intriguing, colorful, and imaginative scores in the history of horse racing.

The horses went to Gerard's farm in Muttontown, New York, for acclimatization. Not long after their arrival, Gerard was dining with friends when a phone call from the farm gave him the sad news that Cinzano (the good horse) had reared up in the shed row, fallen over, and struck his head. He was quite dead.

The doctor decided to forego his crème brûlée, rushed back to the farm, and signed the death certificate for Cinzano.

Now Jack Morgan, whose official identity has always been quite hazy and hardly germane in this abbreviated version, was left with only one horse. Sadly, it was the bad one, Lebon. But fortunately for the owner, he had collected $150,000 on the mortality life insurance claim on the "good" horse, Cinzano. So things could have been worse.

Actually, things were about to get a great deal better. After several months, the pitifully endowed Lebon was entered in a cheap race, going a mile and a quarter on the grass.

Guess what! He romped home by five lengths and paid $116 for a two-dollar ticket. After the race the fifty-dollar cashier's window was a beehive of activity. A certain gentleman had wagered $1,300 to win and $600 to show. His return: he would net $74,000.

Since the cashier did not keep that much lettuce in his drawer, he had to send a runner down to the vault for reserves. It so happened that when the runner — an exercise rider in the mornings — came huffing and puffing up to the window, he spied, and recognized the lucky bettor. It was Dr. Gerard. "Hi ya, Doc. Congratulations!"

It was an unwelcome salutation.

Shortly after that, an avid fan in South America was fascinated by a photo and story in his local newspaper. It told of the spectacular payoff of an ex-Uruguayan horse named Lebon. He perused it carefully and then decided to make a helpful call to the American Jockey Club. He advised officials that the horse in the winner's circle was misidentified. He pointed out that any horseplayer worth his salt would know that this animal was Cinzano, not Lebon.

The elongated star on his forehead was unmistakably that of Cinzano. So, too, did the three-inch scar on his shoulder help in clearing up the unfortunate case of mistaken identity.

Dr. Gerard lost his practice (he had once been the vet for Secretariat) and was sentenced to one year in prison.

Cinzano's papers were lifted, and he was barred for life from racing.

The great sportswriter, Red Smith, commented, "The Doc got a year; the horse got life. Maybe the horse had the wrong lawyer."

THE BET

An astute handicapper made the score of this century (and maybe the last) when Monarchos, Invisible Ink, and Congaree finished in that order in the 2001 Kentucky Derby.

He is Rocco Landesman, and he is a thoroughly delightful man of many facets. He enjoys the distinction of being one of today's most successful producers on the current Broadway scene and is president of a company that owns many of the finest theaters in New York.

Rocco is a gambler's gambler. He possesses sharpness and instinct tinged with genius, the *cojones* to put his money where his brain is, and an easy, resilient nature that gives the impression of one who floats through life having a glorious time, though he lives and thrives in a pressure-cooker world.

Much of the "research" that goes into his horse racing bets is conducted by an unusual man in Rocco's employ, a professional gambler known on the racetrack as "Mr. Dirt." The appellation comes about because this Columbia graduate does not feel strongly that "cleanliness is next to godliness." A high grading in tidiness and personal hygiene was not a prerequisite for the recruitment of Mr. Dirt as a source for pedigree evaluation, workout times, and "inside" information on a wide variety of subjects concerning man and beast.

Rocco bets every day what would be a great deal of money to you and me. These selections are consummated after a phone call to, or personal consultation with, Mr. Dirt.

One of his most noteworthy days occurred in 1993 when, it is said, he bet $15,000 on Colonial Affair to win the Belmont Stakes. Rocco netted $138,000.

But that was chicken feed.

His play in the 2001 Derby was heralded in Liz Smith's column (to Rocco's slight discomfort), and it was a major lunch topic at Sardi's, Gallagher's, '21', and other watering holes of the sporting and theater crowds. Understandably, Rocco has not exactly confirmed the magnitude of his Derby rewards, nor has he denied them. He just gets rather vague when the subject comes up.

He bet a variety of Derby trifectas (as many gamblers do, of course). One combination called for Monarchos to win, Invisible Ink to run second, and Congaree to place third. Monarchos did, and when longshot Invisible Ink nipped Congaree by a nose for second money, it created a trifecta payoff of $12,238.40 for a two-dollar ticket.

Rocco had purchased one hundred of these babies.

He netted close to $1,200,000!

7

Racing Highlights and Lowlights

To help us hone in on the quality of racehorses today, we have Beyer Ratings, Ragozin Sheets, Thoro-Graph figures, performance indices, *Racing Form* consensus points, Breeders' Cup points, and God knows what other "aids." But what makes the game go is mostly in the eye of the beholder. The relative merits of history's big-name horses are a foolish thing to explore and try to establish, but it's fun, so we absolutely must do it.

Was Ruth greater than Cobb? Could Dempsey have whipped Ali? Would Man o' War have defeated Secretariat? If you saw Secretariat win the Belmont, you will go to your grave saying he would have destroyed the first "Big Red." That's the way you want it to be. You don't even want to hear the argument from the other side.

What matters is what you think.

I remember once staying in Ocala, Florida, at Hobeau Farm, where I had been looking at some horses the farm had for sale. The farm manager, Elmer Heubeck, and his wife, Harriet, had a few people for dinner, including Yancey Christmas and his nephew Billy Christmas, both from a famous Maryland horse family.

Yancey, who considered himself the patriarch of the clan, was a crusty, old curmudgeon who would "tell it like it is." (Not always the most endearing quality, I find.)

Yancey trained horses. So did the younger Billy, who at that time *owned* and trained a fine handicap horse named Terrible Tiger. This four-year-old had been campaigning against the best in the East, and while not dominant, he was quite competitive. It was a great time in Billy's life.

During the lunch Yancey (who "knew who the Unknown Soldier was," to use a wonderful old racetrack expression) had expounded on practically every equine subject, including an unsolicited critique of certain members of the Hobeau stallion roster.

"Elmer, that stallion of yours, Duck Dance — he's not gonna make it."

"I wouldn't give you two dead flies for Step Lively! He'll never throw anything decent."

He covered some more of the Hobeau stock (some of the most successful in racing), then he got around to his nephew.

"Billy, that old horse of yours — that Terrible Tiger — he's no hell. He hasn't beat nothin' yet. He's just not much of a horse."

There was an uncomfortable silence at the table. It went on for what seemed like a long time, while Billy kept his eyes on his dinner plate, intent on maintaining proper respect for his elder.

Finally, he looked up, put his utensils down, and stared at Yancey. Very quietly and very movingly, he said, "*He is to me.*"

"He is to me." That's what it's all about.

Having said how fruitless it is to evaluate racehorses, I am now going to evaluate one.

His name was Kelso, and he was the best horse that ever looked through a bridle! To me.

He could do it all, and he did it for so long. There was no question with him about what he should have done or what he would have done. By God, he did it from the time he was three to when he finally quit at age nine — capable even in his twilight years of beating top horses.

He was voted Horse of the Year five straight years.

He sprinted with the sprinters, and he stayed with the stayers. Kelso carried weight — 130 or better twenty-four times! He ran on dirt, in the mud, on the turf, and he didn't give a damn whose racetrack he was asked to run on. He ran in Illinois, New Jersey, California, Florida, Maryland, and, of course, New York. And he was absolute murder everywhere. When you asked Kelso the question, he provided the answer!

I first saw Kelso when he was wintering in Aiken in 1964. Anne and I came over from Atlanta with my mother and father. We had read that the great horse, then seven, would work a half-mile for the public during the Aiken Trials, a delightful exhibition day of racing. On the deep Aiken track, where a half-mile in :49 is noteworthy, the old boy cruised in an eye-popping :47.

Part of his charm to me was his looks. He didn't take your breath away. He was no matinee idol — just a plain brown wrapper. He stood a solid sixteen hands. His head was decent, a trifle too long perhaps, but Kelso's eye was the beacon of his class and quality. And from a conformation standpoint, he would have been unspectacular but awfully hard to fault.

The horse had been gelded at two, when he was on his obstreperous way to being a useless rogue. He was a poster boy for castration. Gelding him saved the day, but he never lost his impish, independent streak. This was demonstrated at the 1964 Washington, D.C., International. Each of the horses had been given a blanket emblazoned with the flag of the nation he was representing, and their connections were asked to bring the horses over from the barns properly adorned. It was part of the wonderful pageantry of that particular race.

Kelso did not care for his blanket. I can still see him, walking down the stretch, wheeling, kicking, and raising hell. Finally, before he "left his race" on the route to the paddock, his handlers removed the blanket, and he walked in to be saddled with complete aplomb.

That may have been the best horse race I have ever witnessed. It was Kelso's fourth attempt to win this mile and a half race on the turf. The horse was now seven, and some said he was past his prime. The ingredients made for an event loaded with drama.

One of the great handicappers of the era was the swashbuckling Gun Bow, who had taken Kelso's measure in both the Brooklyn Handicap and the Woodward Stakes earlier in the fall. Gun Bow, a four-year-old at the top of his game, was also representing America in this race.

And it was strictly a two-horse race. Kelso went off at 1.20 to the dollar and Gun Bow at 1.50. Why was Kelso the shorter price? Because he got good in the fall, and the race was in "Kelly's" hometown, where he had a pretty big fan club.

No fan was more avid than I. I worked for an advertising agency in Atlanta at the time, and I was in charge of a large and important stove account. I had dreamed of going to see this great horse race, but the stove people had their annual sales meeting on the same Saturday. I was presenting the advertising program, so not to be there would be unthinkable.

About two weeks before the sales meeting, the president of my agency and I flew up to the stove company headquarters to give the bigwigs a preview. They liked the material very much, and everything was set for the upcoming sales meeting.

While having lunch with top execs after the preview, Bill Neal, the president of my agency, surprisingly announced, "Fellows, Cot won't be here to present this program at the sales meeting. I'm going to come and do it instead of him. He's a big horse-racing nut, as you know, and one of the greatest races of the year is taking place in Washington that day. And I couldn't let him miss it."

Bill Neal was my great friend, and I have never forgotten him for that (and for a lot of other things). It was probably a dicey thing for him to do, but I loved him for it. The client big shots looked sort of stunned, but they got into the spirit of it and even applauded my going.

So I went to Washington for the race.

Laurel Race Course was packed that day in 1964. Seats were long since sold out, so I tipped an usher five dollars to let me stand in the aisle behind a finish line box. I'm sure I was far more nervous than Kelso's owner, trainer, or jockey.

It was thrilling to see that fine field of racehorses, representing Russia, Ireland, France, Venezuela, Italy, Japan, and, of course, America.

In those days the International used the walk-up start to accommodate the foreigners, and when the field broke, in a pretty orderly manner, it quickly became a two-horse race. Gun Bow powered his way to the lead under Walter Blum, and Kelso stalked a length or two behind him.

They stayed that way for six furlongs. But with the second six furlongs left, Kelso and Milo Valenzuela said to hell with this — let's put him to the test. Kelly ranged up and looked Gun Bow in the eye. Both horses quickened. Gun Bow was not going to relinquish the lead (and he had been running along so easily). Now Kelso had committed and was ready for a long, desperate battle.

By the time they hit the midway point on the backstretch, both great horses had been set down for the drive. What ensued was one hellacious horse race. The crowd went absolutely berserk.

Now, I have always had an unfortunate reflex that kicks in during moments of viewing thrilling physical endeavors. I scream out the oath "goddamn." Not admirable, I know, but if I get stirred up enough, it will happen. I was at this point stirred up.

Standing next to me was a man who felt very strongly about Gun Bow. I didn't particularly care, but just through the osmosis of standing together for several hours, I knew he was a Gun

Bow believer and learned he had come down from New York especially for the race. Conversely, he had to know that I supported Kelso.

With the gauntlet having been thrown down at the three-quarters pole and both horses going at it tooth and nail, this man and I engaged in a weird sort of subconscious dialog that neither of us knew was happening.

As Gun Bow fought to repulse the relentless Kelso, the man would scream out this wishful message, "He's hooked him, but he can't handle him!"

I came back with, "Goddamn, Kelly — you got him now!"

And so it went. The two indomitable warriors were locked in grim combat for a gut-wrenching half-mile, neither giving an inch.

"He's hooked him. But he can't handle him!"

"Goddamn, Kelly — you got him now!"

Something had to give, and Gun Bow did. In mid-stretch, Milo asked Kelso for his life, and the old horse reached back and laid it on the line. It was as if Kelso were saying to Gun Bow, "You'd better put your heart in God…cause your ass is mine!"

Gun Bow cracked. It was Kelso's day. He exuberantly poured it on through the stretch, as if he knew this might be his greatest racing day, and perhaps his last racing day.

He went on to win by four and a half lengths in a new American record time.

Both the Gun Bow man and I were exhausted, wrung out. With no words exchanged before, we were now somehow like old friends. He muttered, "Some damned horse!" We smiled at each other vaguely, stuck out our hands for a shake, and then went our separate ways.

Kelso had hooked him, but he *could* handle him.

Kelso was retired at the start of his nine-year-old season. He fractured a sesamoid while training for a Florida campaign.

He quit the campaign trail for a wonderful life, barnstorming around the country, making public appearances for good causes. He fox hunted, although I do not think he was the most relaxing ride in the hunt field. He exhibited his modest jumping prowess at the National Horse Show in Washington, D.C. When he was not otherwise engaged, he whiled away his years in a lovely paddock at Allaire du Pont's great farm on Maryland's Eastern Shore. Kelso received thousands of visitors, enjoyed his own well-organized fan club, and had a giant mailbox near his paddock to which came a never-ending flow of letters addressed to the old boy.

Kelso went to horse heaven in the ideal manner. At age twenty-six, he was vanned to Belmont so that he could be paraded along with another wonderful old gelding, Forego. The occasion was the running of the Jockey Club Gold Cup and a related benefit for the Thoroughbred Retirement Fund.

When he got back to the farm the next day, Kelso died. It was comparable to a famous old World War II general being honored as grand marshal of a ticker-tape parade down Broadway…and then dying. What a way to go!

After the International, I wrote Allaire asking for some memento of the horse. She replied with a lovely letter and sent me one of his shoes, which I mounted along with her letter.

Allaire du Pont was the ideal owner for the horse, and her personality had much to do with creating the wonderful aura that surrounded what was "the best horse that ever looked through a bridle." To me, that is.

Greyhound

I've seen just about every great American Thoroughbred racehorse of the last half of the twentieth century, on the track or in retirement. I do love the runners, but I must say not many have thrilled me more than did the Standardbred horse Greyhound one summer day in a little town in central Missouri.

Chapter 7

He was a majestic, high-headed gray gelding who raced until he was eight and lived until he was thirty-three. His heyday was in the thirties, when the racing of horses was a sport foremost on the mind of America. It was not unusual years ago for big crowds to turn out just to watch a train go by, if it was hauling a famous racehorse. Think of that! Racehorses were national heroes, and many products and services paid dearly for use of their names — Dan Patch, Twenty Grand, Seabiscuit, Man o' War, and Greyhound.

During his life Greyhound established fourteen world trotting records, not the least of which was a mile in 1:55¼, which he set in 1938 when he was in his natural prime.

In August of that year, at the Missouri State Fair in Sedalia, he sought to break the record for a mile on a half-mile track and would trot against the clock in a public exhibition on the hard, swift oval there.

I was eleven years old and was in Sedalia with my parents for the state championship Saddle Horse show, one of the finest in the Midwest. It was announced that Greyhound would attempt to establish a new world record and that the event would take place "in late afternoon" on Wednesday, with all fair-goers invited to see this "gratis attraction."

Greyhound had been stabled for a week in one of the show horse barns, so for several days before the big day, I, along with some of our Shoestring Stable grooms, would find excuses to walk by his stall. Much of the time it was draped with heavy wrapping paper to give the horse some rest and relaxation from us rubes. But late each morning he went out to train, and I was always on hand when the harness was put on him. His well-known driver-trainer, Sep Palin, would take the reins and slip into the sulky seat under Greyhound's big white rump. Then they would amble out to the track, with scores of people following to watch Greyhound jog…and jog…and jog — as trotters and pacers do.

The day came, and great electricity filled the town and the fairgrounds. By mid-afternoon few people were viewing the poultry or watching the Holstein heifer judging or looking for the "frog boy" at the freak show on the midway. At noon the loud speaker began periodic announcements that Greyhound, "the greatest trotting horse the world has ever known," would trot against the clock at four o'clock. By 3:30 you could have shot a cannon through the midway and not hit a soul.

A steady stream of humanity trekked toward the track. This facility was pretty simple, consisting of a fairly narrow oval with an inside and outside rail, with a crude judges' stand at the finish line. The stand on this day was heavily inhabited by men in shirtsleeves and straw hats, with red, beribboned badges identifying them as judges, announcer, and, more importantly, clockers. There was a small set of bleachers with a roof, suitable perhaps for two hundred. This was filled by the mayor of Sedalia, the lieutenant governor of the state, and various other dignitaries and big shots in the Standardbred world.

The viewing area for us who were uncredentialed was simply a large, grassy bank sloped like a levee. You just found a spot and sat down.

I went over to the track with our trainer, a couple of grooms, and a local blacksmith. It was hot as blazes, and we sat there for the longest time. Finally, a murmur went through the crowd. People began pointing down the path toward the barn area. There, a cloud of dust signaled the approach of Greyhound and his entourage.

Sep Palin drove him up to the judges' stand and turned him toward the crowd. A groom took the checkrein from the horse's withers so Greyhound could relax during the introduction. The gelding stood quietly in the heat while the announcer detailed the big gray's accomplishments and impressed upon us that we were about to see history made.

"Put your hands together for the mighty Greyhound and his legendary driver, Sep Palin," he instructed. We clapped like hell.

We were told Greyhound would make three warm-up laps; on the last, when the flag dropped, he would commence his trot for the world record. He would go twice around, and three clockers would certify his run.

Sep tipped his cap, the checkrein was reattached, and off they jogged.

There must have been three thousand spectators on that bank, and we were revved up. When Greyhound and Sep came by on their first warm-up lap, we all cheered mightily. We did it again on the second round.

When he hit the last stretch turn before the start, you could see old Sep settle his rear end into the seat, shrug his shoulders, and lean forward to get a new purchase on the reins. The team picked up tempo as they came through the stretch. The run hadn't started yet, but we were going crazy. The flag dropped at the wire, Sep popped that big whip to let Greyhound know it was time to go to work, and the run was on.

Down the backstretch they continued. Now, strangely enough, the crowd made not a sound. The only thing audible was the thrilling, thunderous tattoo of the hooves of that great trotting horse. You could have heard that in downtown Sedalia.

As Greyhound came through the turn and swept into the stretch, he looked like he was at a forty-five-degree angle. Sep, flicking that whip dramatically over his back — but not touching him — was leaning in so far his head looked in danger of scraping the rail! When they came spinning out of the turn, the incredible pace seemed to accelerate.

What a sight!

I will never forget what happened then. A black man in overalls was sitting about ten feet over to my left. As Greyhound came toward us with his furious rush, that man slowly got to his feet, almost in shock and wonderment. He grabbed the felt hat off his head, crushed it into his hand and screamed out, "Gawd a mighty — *damn*!!!"

That gray horse was picking 'em up and laying 'em down as he went through his second lap.

We didn't know how he stood with the clock, and we really didn't care. At this point every human being present, including the halt, the sick, and the lame, was on his feet screaming — just for the sheer, by God, exhilaration of it! How could you help it?

Greyhound finished all out, with his old head straining out in front of him as he fought to find that wire. He might not have known about any world record, but he knew what he was born, bred, and trained to do. And he knew, I am convinced, that no other could do it better.

We gave him a deafening reception as he went past. Sep then slowed him gradually and trotted around another lap, rather than stopping and turning him. As Greyhound came by us, Sep doffed his cap, then acknowledged the applause with his whip. He stopped the horse in front of the judges' stand. The groom quickly unchecked him. An unidentified lady suddenly ran out and kissed him on the nose.

Then the announcer informed us, "Greyhound trotted in two oh one and two (2:01.2), missing the world record for a mile on a half-mile track by only one second. Let's hear it for the immortal Greyhound and his driver, Sep Palin!"

Did they hear it! The world record would have been nice, but no one on that grassy bank at those old-time fairgrounds in Sedalia, Missouri, would ever forget one of the truly magical moments of our lives.

Gawd a mighty — *damn*!

Summer Squall and Unbridled

Unbridled, that superb racehorse and sire, has just died —

as I write this. He and Summer Squall, Dogwood's pride and joy, dominated the three-year-old crop of 1990. They were the keenest of rivals in as friendly a fashion as fierce competition can permit. Unbridled was trained by Carl Nafzger and our horse by the superb Neil Howard. We were all friends and never let rivalry get out of hand.

The two horses met six times. Summer Squall finished in front of Unbridled four times and lost twice to him. Yet Unbridled ended up winning more than twice as much money as our horse ($4,489,475 versus $1,844,282). Unbridled won the Kentucky Derby and the Breeders' Cup Classic. He was named champion, and he should have been.

We beat him in the Blue Grass Stakes. After our second to him in the Derby, we went to Baltimore and defeated him in the Preakness.

Now the logical Triple Crown rubber match was the Belmont Stakes. However, our horse was a bleeder, and we could not use the anti-bleeding diuretic medication Lasix in New York. Therefore, we opted not to run, even though whichever horse — Unbridled or Summer Squall — finished best in that race would receive a million-dollar bonus. Unbridled, also a bleeder, did run in the Belmont, finishing fourth. So he backed into the big dough. (I always kidded Carl Nafzger that he should have given Dogwood a ten percent commission.)

We rested until September, won the Pennsylvania Derby, and then headed for Bossier City, Louisiana, for the million-dollar Super Derby. Unbridled had the same race on his dance card.

Here, then, was your rubber match.

With the race at Louisiana Downs set for a Sunday, Summer Squall arrived by plane with Unbridled and some other runners on Wednesday. He settled in nicely, went to the racetrack for a gallop on Thursday, and could not have looked better. He trained again Friday morning and went fine.

I arrived in Shreveport that morning, went by the barn to check on the horse and then went to my motel. That afternoon at feeding time I returned to the barn.

I pulled up to the stakes barn, where I noticed Neil and two veterinarians at the door of the horse's stall. As I approached, several sportswriters stopped me. While I talked to them, I glanced over at Neil, who impatiently motioned me over. I did not like the looks of that. I brought the interview to a close, and with as much nonchalance as I could force, I sauntered over to Summer Squall's stall.

"Horse has got a temperature. Not much. Took it an hour ago, and it was 102 and change. It may not amount to anything. Might have gotten stirred up or something. Dr. Norwood is going to take it again in a few minutes," Neil said.

We waited fifteen minutes. The thermometer said 101.4. Going down. We took Squall's temperature again in another hour, and it was normal. We all breathed a sigh of relief. Just a fluke.

Summer Squall galloped like a champ on Saturday morning. His temperature stayed right at normal. Clearly, we were out of the woods.

At noon I went to the Shreveport Airport to pick up Anne and our friend Helen Brann, flying in from Atlanta. I told them about the scare, and we all speculated on how horrible it would have been to scratch the horse.

Squall was one of six three-year-olds owned by a large Dogwood partnership of twenty-eight shares. Many of these partners were either already in Shreveport or well on the way.

Not only that, but the 1990 Super Derby was shaping up as the race of the year, with the two big contenders vying for divisional leadership. The racetrack had promoted the daylights out of the race, and there wasn't a hotel room available within fifty miles. Louisiana Downs had long since sold out of reserved seats. Never before had the demand for press credentials been so great. It figured to be the biggest and most important day in the track's history.

The three of us had lunch and then went back to the motel. As Anne and I walked into the room, I noticed the dreaded red light on the phone blinking away. The message center told me to "call Neil Howard at the barn." Oh Lord!

"Maybe you'd better come on out here," Neil suggested.

I did. When I got to the barn, a rather forlorn little cluster had assembled outside the stall: two vets, Neil Howard, and Squall's fine groom, Willie. An aggregation of sportswriters sniffed around in the vicinity, so we all went in the stall with the colt.

"Temperature's 102," Neil said, rolling his eyes.

I looked at Dr. Gary Norwood. He shrugged, "I don't know what to tell you. He doesn't *seem* sick. The temperature may not have any significance, and he might run fine. But it's gone up again. Your call."

I told Neil, "Let's take a ride." We got in my car and drove around the barn area.

The trainer said, "Well, we've come a long way. But I know one thing. It's not like him to carry a temperature of 102, and he's shown us that twice in two days."

We bypassed the prestigious Belmont Stakes and kissed off a chance at a million-dollar bonus just because we couldn't run on Lasix. We've got the Meadowlands Cup coming up, and after that, the gold ring — the Breeders' Cup Classic at two million dollars. And our horse is definitely not one hundred percent going into this race.

If we scratch, we're going to decimate the race of the year, Louisiana Downs is going to lose hundreds of thousands of dollars, and all the Dogwood partners are going to be devastated. Not an easy decision.

"We've got to scratch him," I told Neil. He sighed with relief.

"Don't say a word to anyone, vets included. I've got to talk to Edward DeBartolo (owner of the racetrack) as soon as possible. They're having that big party tonight, and I've got to find out how he wants to handle this," I told Neil.

I called the racing secretary and told him I needed to meet with him and his boss as quickly as possible.

"Mr. DeBartolo is still in his suite in his skybox on the top floor of the grandstand. Since the party starts at six, he just stayed at the track. I'll meet you up there in a few minutes, unless it's something I can handle," he told me.

"We need him in on this," I explained.

When I got to the skybox, the nervous racing secretary was there. DeBartolo jumped to his feet, gave me a big grin, shook hands, and said cheerily, "Hello, Cot, my good man. Whatever can I do for you? Are we treating you right? (chuckle)" He thought maybe I needed more seats or something.

"I've got to scratch our horse — Summer Squall. He's sick."

His reply was heartfelt and got right to the point.

"Shit!"

"My sentiments exactly," I told him.

"Oh my God," said the racing secretary.

We discussed the situation, and I gave DeBartolo all the details.

"Who knows about this?" he asked.

"The three of us and Neil Howard," I replied.

"Okay, here's what you got to do for me. The deadline for the Sunday papers is eight tonight. I don't want this to get out until the papers have gone to bed, and I'd really like to keep it under wraps until it's too late for TV news at ten. Can you keep it quiet until then? If we don't, I'm going to lose the biggest day in our history," DeBartolo asked.

"Okay, I'll do my damndest, but I'm going to have to tell my partners. A lot of them are coming to the party in about an hour. I'll ask them to play along, but I can't promise a thing. I'm coming to the party, of course, but I'm going to be as late as I can get away with," I said.

What ensued was about the toughest three hours of my life. We did go to the party. By the time we got there, certain members of the press were beginning to smell a rat. I played along with the party line and should have been nominated for an Academy Award for the "best performance by an actor whose heart wasn't in it." I'm sure some of the partners spilled the beans later in the evening. The Dallas paper did have Summer Squall's scratch, but that was the only paper.

As soon as Anne and I could blow that function, we did. We stopped by the barn on our way back to the motel. Summer Squall was at his stall door, as bright as a penny.

I could have killed him! If you're sick, the least you can do is to look sick!

Early the next morning we chartered a plane and got out of there.

Unbridled ran second in that Super Derby but then went on and won the Breeders' Cup and clinched the championship.

Our horse had a virus all fall. He wasn't right until the following April when he started his four-year-old campaign with an allowance win at Keeneland.

8

Mistakes Were Made...

The racing game is streaky; it's a roller coaster ride. Things are either going beautifully, or they are going to hell in a hand basket. Much of the time there seems to be a decided drift toward the latter! But both conditions can change abruptly.

In the heat of horse races, split-second decisions, often flawed, are made. Chances for miscalculations are enhanced considerably when the sporting endeavor involves a dozen gigantic animals going lickety-split!

And then, as in life generally, there are simply days, situations, and people that are star-crossed.

This chapter deals with errant decisions, bonehead plays, and dismal days. All have a humorous slant...now, that is.

Pilot Errors

Bill Shoemaker, considered by many to be our all-time greatest jockey, will also go down in history as poster boy for the highest-visibility mistake in the annals of racing — a blunder the greenest of green apprentice riders would not have committed.

He was going to win the Kentucky Derby on Gallant Man in 1957 when he mistook the sixteenth pole for the finish line. He stood up in the irons, squandering his momentum, before the arrival of the wire. He finished second to Iron Liege.

Eddie Arcaro — Steady Eddie, and arguably America's premier jockey of the forties and fifties — badly misjudged the distance of the Pimlico Cup. He thought the race was one and one-half miles. It was two and one-half miles. He eased his horse the second time he hit the finish line. It should have been the third!

While Arcaro and Shoemaker made famous miscalculations, Sylvester Carmouche made an infamously calculated move that backfired. A Cajun rider hardly in the same league with Shoemaker or Arcaro, Carmouche dealt his career a severe blow with his creativity.

He was banned from racing in 1990 for ten years after taking a shortcut on a fog-shrouded day in a mile race at Delta Downs. He was aboard a 23-1 longshot named Landing Officer.

When the starter sent the horses on their way at the top of the stretch, sly Sylvester simply took hold of his horse, stopped him, waited patiently, and when he heard the field coming around the turn (he certainly could not *see* them in the pea-soup fog) he clucked to Landing Officer, put him into a spirited gallop, and won the race by twenty-four lengths. It appeared a flagrant reversal of form, and no one was fooled.

It was not a red-letter day in the life of the young Cajun jockey. I think, though, that I would have enthusiastically traded places with him on my own day of torture — June 29, 1991.

Horrors of Hollywood Park

Gruesome is a euphemistic adjective for that day in California that "will live in infamy." Ironically, it emanated from one of the greatest sources of pleasure in my lifetime: Summer Squall. If ever, after years and years of sobriety, I had been inclined to seek solace again from demon rum, this ghastly day would have been the logical opportunity.

The occasion was the running of the million-dollar Hollywood Gold Cup.

I will set the stage. Summer Squall's four-year-old campaign began, after a winter in Aiken, with an allowance win at Keeneland. After this six and a half-furlong sprint race, I felt he needed to run in a middle-distance stake at Keeneland for maximum fitness before we tackled the highly contentious Pimlico Special at one mile and three-sixteenths. I let myself be talked out of it.

As I feared, the horse was not tight enough, and Farma Way beat him at Pimlico. We were second.

We came back at Churchill Downs in early June with another allowance win and then shipped to Los Angeles for the Gold Cup, a race for which we would be favored.

Now, let us depart from the narrative and point out that one reason Dogwood Stable forms only four-share general partnerships today is because of Summer Squall. The inevitable pressure of managing a high-profile, glamour horse owned by twenty-eight different partners was a colossal pain in the ass! Actually, there were forty shares offered in a six-horse package, but, thank the good Lord, several kind souls took multiple shares, cutting down on the number of human beings involved. Still, there were far too many if one wished to preserve one's sanity. And, understandably, they all wanted to see the horse run and wanted to bring family and friends!

We started off advising the partners that we would do our best to make arrangements for them at the racetracks. However, we asked that they understand there were twenty-eight partners and we would appreciate it if they would try to fend for themselves. There was not much "fending," and it was quickly apparent that from a practical standpoint we were better off handling their racetrack accommodations. The alternative was for them to ask us what to do, be disgruntled about it, and screw things up royally with the racetrack.

Naturally, with the horse looking like he was going to

slaughter the competition during the rest of the year and become champion, everybody and his dog wanted to go to Hollywood Park for the first big step.

Neil Howard, Willie Woods (groom), and Robert Vickers (exercise rider) flew out with Squall a week ahead of the event. Anne and I went out on Tuesday before the Saturday race. We stayed at the glamorous Bel Air Hotel. Not bad digs, but an hour's drive from the racetrack (if you made the journey at 3 a.m.!).

Our first morning there, an earthquake started us off in a memorable manner. And I don't mean a tremor or two; we had a bona fide earthquake around seven. In fact, a racetrack employee died when a steel beam fell in the grandstand and crushed him. The aftershocks had caused some confusion in the barns, but our horse was fine. His connections were pretty nervous (not having their origins in earthquake land).

Then Friday morning after Summer Squall had trained for the last time before the next day's Gold Cup, Neil, Robert, and I were standing outside his stall, probably contemplating the onslaught of another quake. Willie was doing him up, and we heard him say, "Y'all better come on in here." More good news *à la* Louisiana Downs?

Willie picked up his hoof, took his brush, and hit a few licks across the horse's heel. There, big as life, was a crack from the fleshy coronet band about two inches down into his hoof. A dreaded quarter crack. To the uninitiated, this malady on a horse would be like a pianist trying to play the tempestuous *Flight of the Bumblebee* with a split fingernail. A horrendous problem for a horse getting ready to run a mile and a quarter against the world's best.

The blacksmith was summoned. He inspected the foot, didn't think it was too bad, and suggested that we gallop Summer Squall the next morning (the day of the race, mind you). If he moved well over the track with weight on him, then he was a good candidate to run. In the meantime he would be tubbed in a solution to ease the soreness.

With the race right on us, Summer Squall owners, press, and the general public seemed to be wandering through the barn in droves. What the hell were we to tell them about why the horse was virtually living in a tub of turpentine. "Oh…standard procedure…do that before every race," was the vague explanation. As if, "doesn't everybody follow this practice?" More than a few sensed that this was a trifle strange.

When you have a big horse, life becomes more complicated, and it is often in the best interests of all concerned to lie a little bit. The last thing we needed at this point was to start spreading the word that Summer Squall had a quarter crack. We certainly did not need a committee meeting to deal with it.

Saturday morning we put the tack on Summer Squall, and he went once around. Robert reported afterward, "No problem. Same old Squall."

We would run.

The Dogwood connections needed accommodations at the racetrack, at final count, for a total of thirty-eight.

The brunt of making prior (long-distance) arrangements for this unwieldy number fell to Jack Sadler, Dogwood's long-suffering "communications director." The job of on-site social director was mine, with able assistance from the indefatigable Anne.

Despite the fact that there were nine horses running — three owned by large partnerships! — the Hollywood Park people gave us two tables for twelve in the turf club. That took care of twenty-four. They also gave us a box for six, and I scrounged another box for eight from a California friend.

Amazingly, there are always a few people who decide blithely at the last minute to bring other guests, figuring it will work out some way. But then there are also some no-shows (my absolute favorite category!). Thus, it should even out.

Our carefully orchestrated plan of fairness was to put the best clients, the ones with the most longevity, in the turf club at the tables. The others were to be assigned to the boxes. The names of every party and the designation "turf club" or "box" were left at the "will call" window at the clubhouse entrance. Everything seemed to be under control.

Interestingly, at that time the young lady in charge of horsemen's relations was Jenine Sahadi. She is today one of the most respected horse trainers in the country. Difficult though horse training may be, I am sure she sought a haven in that relatively tranquil vocation after experiencing the rigors of dealing with the owners for the Hollywood Gold Cup of 1991.

About 12:30 the Dogwoodites began arriving at the turf club where Anne and I were on duty. The box seat people were simply to go to their assigned boxes, sit down, and not be heard from, presumably. It was assumed that they would never know and brood about the more glamorous amenities above them.

Oddly, some people arriving at the turf club I could have sworn I had assigned to boxes. But I could have been mistaken. Soon we had filled up the two tables. And then I noticed that a third table of twelve was filling up rapidly with Dogwood people. Those in charge seemed to find no fault with this, and I decided not to examine too closely the developments concerning this unexpected third table. I subconsciously explained it away to myself with, "How sweet of Jenine to go the extra mile. Must have been the drawing power of Summer Squall!"

When a client I loathed with great fervor came in with her escort and two unexpected guests, I became quite uneasy. She had definitely been assigned a box, with no deal for lunch. It was now becoming increasingly clear that anyone even remotely associated with Dogwood was being sent up to the Hollywood Turf Club. The individual names left so meticulously at "will call" had obviously been discarded, and now "Dogwood" was the magic name for turf club admittance.

But what the hell! We'd somehow latched on to the extra table. I was not going to sweat it. Some of us would go down and occupy the boxes later in the day.

At this point thirty-six people were lunching contentedly at the three tables, and the rest of the dining area was tightly packed with the connections of the other horses. I was going to be a hero.

But suddenly a vortex of confusion developed. Jenine, several assistants, and two headwaiters were consulting clipboards and looking frantically around the room. And there were now quite a few would-be diners standing around looking grouchy.

The staff personnel moved over toward Dogwoodland, looked over our three dozen happy campers munching away at three different tables, and then Jenine focused on me. Somehow, I sensed a crisis in the making.

"My God, Cot, your people took a table that was supposed to be for Nedlaw Stable and Clover Racing!

"Oh, we thought that table was ours. Didn't it have a Dogwood sign on it?" I offered lamely, thinking she would figure out a way to work it out.

I was mistaken. "They'll have to move," she announced.

"Are you kidding? They're right in the middle of lunch! Can't you bring in some more tables?" I asked.

"No chance! There's no room for any more tables. I'm sorry. I told you that you had two tables, and you're occupying three! Those people have got to go. Come on! This table (around which staff and rightful occupants were now hovering ominously) belongs to Nedlaw and Clover," Jenine laid it right on the line.

There was no choice. It was now my unenviable task to go to the twelve diners at table number three, tell them to stop eating, stand up, and leave the turf club. And, wouldn't you know, the client for whom I had a hearty dislike had somehow infiltrated herself and guests into one of the legitimate tables. There was no way I could have singled them out for eviction, in which I would have taken some pleasure.

So, I gritted my teeth and started. I moved my way down the table, apologizing and asking them to get up immediately and go to the empty boxes (whose locations only "will call" knew!). By this time, the other Dogwood people had gotten into the spirit of the fracas and were complaining of this inhumane treatment and offering numerous, unwelcome suggestions. This only added to the confusion. Very slowly, the table was freed (some of the evictees had a little age on them and little enthusiasm for the new plan and did not move with much alacrity).

At this point I was easily the most unpopular person in the room. Nay, in Hollywood Park, if not Southern California! My own partners, the Hollywood Turf Club authorities, and the tardily seated Nedlaw and Clover connections were all mad at me.

All the evictees and I caught the elevator down to "will call" and sorted out box assignments. Box tabs were distributed, and off the people went to find their boxes and sit midst considerable grumbling about where they might find a suitable place to resume their rudely interrupted midday meal.

Mercifully, this wretched "snafu" was drawing to a close. Perhaps the rest of the afternoon would be smoother (it could not help but be), and if we won the race, this would all seem like an amusing little hiccup. We would all chuckle genially about it.

In the grandstand I grabbed a hot dog to go, stuck it in my pocket, and went back up to the turf club to "enjoy" it. I was standing over in the corner of the room choking down this morsel (I certainly had no seat).

Suddenly, out of the elevator burst this very large young woman, the wife of a Dogwood partner. She made straight for me, and she had blood in her eye.

"I heard *you* were up here," she said accusingly. "We were

told that our family — my husband and I, our two daughters, and the baby and his nanny — would have a nice box for the afternoon."

"Do you not?" I asked.

"Well, we're in a box for eight; and with our stroller and two other outside people in the box it's impossibly crowded. And, do you know that we're in a box with two *colored men*!" she shrieked.

It was here that I completely lost it. The earthquake, the quarter crack, the luncheon screwup all combined to cause me to go dangerously close to berserk.

"Madame, the fact that there are 'colored men' in your box is a matter of supreme indifference to me. I would not give a good goddamn if Adolph Hitler and Mussolini were your box mates. If I were you, I would go sit in it and be delighted that on this day you have it," I said.

She could see that I was on the verge of apoplexy and that it was fruitless to pursue the matter further. She left.

The day crept ever so slowly toward 4:30, when the horses would come into the paddock. The next crisis I could foresee would revolve around who would be permitted in the paddock.

I had been given twelve paddock passes, so twenty-six people did not have these credentials for admittance to the saddling area. I handled this problem by acting as if it did not exist. When asked by partners about going to the paddock, I told them where it was, and — coward that I had become — that they were welcome to go to it.

But the proper chronology of the afternoon would have to include that around two o'clock I was paged and told to report to the racing secretary's office. More good news, I was sure. Arriving there, I was sent to the licensing bureau. A very stupid gentleman there asked me for the licenses of the twenty-eight people who owned "the five horse in the stake."

I spent about a half-hour, sweating bullets all the while, explaining to him that Dogwood circumvented that problem by leasing the horse from the partnership. Therefore, the only necessary licensee was me, and I showed him *my* license. He made about five phone calls and then said, "Okay, I guess it's all right."

At this point my outlook was, "O, Death, where is thy sting?"

In the paddock I tried to make myself invisible to any who might have been refused admittance and would want me to escort them in. Fortunately, the paddock did not have very tight security, and whoever wanted in got in.

Summer Squall arrived, looked terrific, and all seemed well. Pat Day, fresh from Kentucky, strode in, shook a lot of hands, and then was tossed up onto the horse.

Anne, Neil, and I watched the race together, less confident than usual because of the foot situation.

The race was promising for the first seven-eighths of a mile, with Squall laying fourth, behind the pace-making Marquetry. The hammer seemed to be cocked, and it was almost time to pull the trigger. In the middle of the final turn, the real race began. Pat asked our colt for his run, and for a sixteenth of a mile he got it. Then, sickeningly, Squall began to flatten out, shortening stride. He fought, because he was born to fight, but the pain in his foot, when put under extreme pressure, was nullifying his fluid stride. He finished seventh, beaten by about sixteen lengths.

It was clear to those of us who knew what the deal was. However, it did not seem to be a good time to explain to the rest of the partnership our theory of defeat. I had, of course, discussed the situation earlier with my very savvy, longtime partner, Paul Oreffice, but no one else.

There was a post-race party in the beloved turf club following the race, and it behooved us to attend. I hate getting beat, but I have never left a racetrack with anything but a smile on my face, no matter what. This day tested that philosophy of sportsmanship rather severely, but attend we did. It was the end of a perfect day.

We found our driver, went back to the barn, and checked on the horse. Essentially he was fine, except for being mad as hell that he had been whipped. After a few desultory minutes there, we began the torturous, tedious, forlorn, dispirited — you name it, if it's negative — drive back to the Bel Air.

With us was our old friend and Summer Squall partner, Helen Brann, a very erudite and witty woman. We rode along in silence for about fifteen minutes; then she turned toward Anne and me and said, leaning on the lyrics of the great Rodgers and Hart show tune, "The Lady is a Tramp":

"Hate California…it's cold and it's damp."

The only good thing about this day was that it was soon to be over.

Birmingham Turf Club

While we're on the subject of "snafued" situations, we must pay tribute to the first year of operations at the Birmingham Turf Club, an organization that failed miserably and has been for some years virtually defunct.

A consulting economic guru, who later had an ownership position in this Alabama racetrack, developed a very promising financial pro forma for building a Thoroughbred track in Birmingham. Legislators, armed with this ammunition and brimming with competitive spirit focused at besting the neighboring state of Georgia, legalized pari-mutuel wagering in Alabama. This enabled the creation of the Birmingham Turf Club.

One of Alabama's most successful businessmen financed it. He then arranged for his daughter (and the consultant) to own and operate it. Wisely, they hired a racing executive with impeccable credentials. This was Austin Brown, in retirement in

Camden, South Carolina, and a man of impressive racetrack business acumen.

Unfortunately for Brown, Alabama, and horse racing, his managerial talents were completely nullified, in my opinion, by the heavy-handed interference and horrendous blunders of the owners. The result was, despite Brown's well-intentioned efforts, a disastrous, but often amusing, chapter in the annals of racing.

Dogwood was overjoyed with having what looked like first-class facilities within two hours of our hometown (Atlanta, at the time). We committed a sizeable string of eighteen horses to race there when the Birmingham Turf Club opened in March of 1987.

There was to be night racing, and the financial blueprint was predicated on the important projection that one-fourth of the attendance would come from neighboring Georgia, specifically the significant Atlanta market. The gambling-starved Atlantans would come stampeding across the line. You could leave Atlanta at six (Eastern time) and be having dinner in the extremely sumptuous turf club dining room when the first race went off at 7:30! It only took two hours to get there, and you could gain an hour going over. Right! But you lost it going back, which means if you stayed for the feature race at 10:30, you got home at 1:30 in the morning. A trifle tough when you had to get up the next morning.

First mistake. Not for very long did Atlantans stampede across the state line.

The turf club dining room was very large, very elegant, and very expensive. And very sparsely populated!

The backbone of the racetrack, the blue-collar workers, of which there were plenty in Birmingham, found that by the time they had parked their car, paid to get in, bought a program, and then splurged for a hot dog and a beer, they had done serious damage to a double sawbuck. They began finding other amusements.

The horsemen had a few complaints. They always do, but in Birmingham their bitching was well founded.

Opening night, the track put on a $50,000 stake for fillies and mares, going a mile and one-sixteenth on the dirt. Because it was opening night, management decided to follow the opening ceremonies with the feature race. The mayor and other city and state dignitaries were on hand to salute this new sport for the state, the track's owners spoke, and the ribbon separating the racetrack and the paddock was cut. The presentations were strategically timed so that at their zenith the fine field of fillies and mares would start the walk around the racetrack and make their way into the paddock.

After the high school band that had been honored with this assignment concluded its rousing rendition of "Stars Fell on Alabama," the first field of Thoroughbred racehorses ever to compete in Alabama was to arrive at the paddock.

Everything was going fine, and the distaffers were nearing the entrance to the paddock in relative orderliness. However, at that moment the band director decided that, while the first, fairly tame number had been well received, "Alabamy Bound" would really show the crowd a thing or two. With staggering volume and zest, the Panthers Marching Band let it all hang out!

Well, these race mares were stakes campaigners, seasoned, and not by any means lacking in poise. But when the Panthers' vaunted brass section hit its best musical stride on their signature number, all hell broke loose. Loose horses galloped in every direction, and grooms quickly littered the paddock.

The poor paddock judge was finally able to shush the band, and the horses were gradually recaptured (a few were on their way back to the barns!).

One of the track owners, long associated with Alabama's most successful motor speedway, had taken a page from auto racing protocol and unwisely arranged for a fireworks display to salute the dawn of an auspicious new era in Alabama sports.

It was to be a "silent" fireworks display.

It now began. But, alas, it was not silent.

Just as "Alabamy Bound" was mercifully brought under control, there was launched what seemed to be an authentic reenactment of the U.S. Navy's Third Fleet bombardment of Okinawa.

Those horses that had been caught took off again. There was no way to stop the fireworks extravaganza, and it seemed interminable. It certainly was to me. We were running a wonderfully reliable mare named Natania, who had the disposition and prerace animation of a milk cow. She had not offered to break from her stout groom, but she *was* by this time wringing wet.

All of this necessitated a fifteen-minute delay of the post parade for the first race. "The Star-Spangled Banner" (the only thing possibly left to render) was aborted when Austin Brown was permitted to make an executive decision.

The field went off with two vet scratches. Natania closed well to get second money, and we were lucky to settle for it.

But if there were glitches on the front side, the backside brought new meaning to the term.

One of the most interesting developments had to do with toilet facilities. Birmingham Turf Club barns housed about one thousand horses. Fine. But with this many animals, there would have to be numerous human beings to ride, groom, and train those horses. And it followed that these people would definitely need to go to the bathroom from time to time.

Very cleverly, the dormitories were designed to include plumbing facilities.

However, in the master construction plan there were no public toilets anywhere on the backstretch. Without drawing you a picture, this did present a retardant to the efficiency of the workday. If a barn employee or visitor wished to go to the bathroom, he or she either had to visit his or her dormitory room (if the employee was housed on the track; and many were not) or trek to the racing office, a half-mile away from some far-flung barns. There were bathrooms for each gender at that site, but they were designed to accommodate a small coterie of office personnel.

You could hardly gain admittance to the racing secretary's office to enter your horse, as the lines of antsy people yearning to use the bathroom snaked throughout most of the building. A urinal manufacturer seeking testimonials to the durability of its product would have found Birmingham Turf Club an ideal test site.

Another unusual design involved the mechanical hot-walking machines adjacent to every barn. This labor-saving equipment is — for those neophyte readers — simply an axis from which long arms extend, and it rotates slowly. Thus, four horses are hooked on after training and made to walk and cool out, freeing up a human being (a hotwalker) to perform other duties (look for a bathroom perhaps?).

The terrain around Birmingham is hilly, and in many cases the ground adjacent to a barn had been built up by earthmoving equipment and then graded for smoothness. In a few cases the graders had been somewhat stingy with the amount of ground provided, and many of these bases fell off sharply. Some of the hotwalking machines were positioned perilously close to a virtual "cliff."

As long as the horse walked sedately around the perimeter, there was no problem. However, if he wheeled his hind end away from the machine and kicked out in a fit of exuberance, there would be no earth when his rear legs came back toward earth! He would find his hind end dangling over the cliff. Several animals developed a distinct concern about walking machines as a result of life in Birmingham.

But the *pièce de résistance* concerning the unenlightened personnel of the Birmingham racetrack came in the director of admissions' office on the second night of operations.

A surprisingly large crowd came through the turnstiles on night number two. Unfortunately, an insufficient number of programs containing that night's entries had been ordered.

In a panic, the program sellers phoned the admissions office.

"We've run out of programs. What should we do?"

Answer: "Don't worry. We've got plenty left over from last night. I'll send them right down to you!"

Tipping My Hat (Or, Being Polite Doesn't Pay)

Some years ago I breezed into the paddock before a race at Keeneland, feeling rather full of myself. There I encountered a friend, Brereton Jones, a well-known racing personality who later became governor of Kentucky.

Brery was part of a group of four or five people. Included were a distinguished gentleman of international acclaim and his very elegant wife. I had not met this couple, who were new to racing but in the process of developing a major racing and breeding operation. I felt that I should meet them.

I sauntered over to the group and thrust myself into the conversation in what I am afraid was a rather heavy-handed manner. I shook hands with my friend Brery Jones, and he, of course, introduced me to the couple I had targeted.

Now I must digress here to point out that for much of my life it has been my custom to wear a hat — either a felt fedora *hat* or an English tweed *cap.* And when I was a very small boy, my father told me always to remove, or tip, my hat when encountering or being introduced to a lady. I have not remembered everything my father told me, but I have been steadfast about this.

So, as I was introduced to the big shot and his wife, I gave forth my most ingratiating smile. With my eyes twinkling with

On the surface, Birmingham Turf Club seemed too good to be true — and it was. Angel Penna, shown with the author and jockey Jean Cruguet, had a unique way of communicating but always made his point.

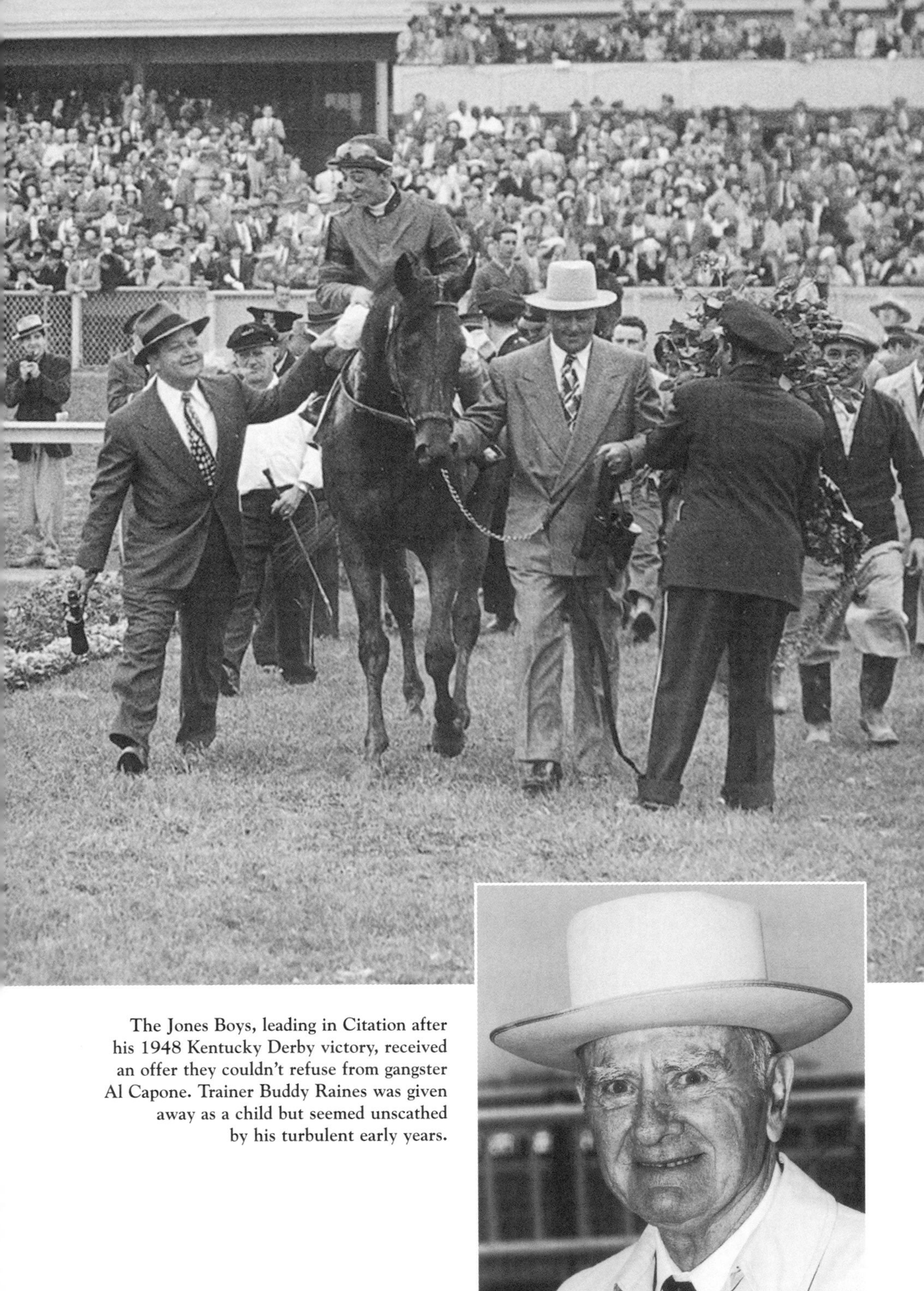

The Jones Boys, leading in Citation after his 1948 Kentucky Derby victory, received an offer they couldn't refuse from gangster Al Capone. Trainer Buddy Raines was given away as a child but seemed unscathed by his turbulent early years.

Beneath the stern exterior of trainer Whistling Bob Smith (above) lay a penchant for *The Lone Ranger* radio series. Leslie Combs, the irrepressible master of Spendthrift Farm, could charm the birds out of the trees or the money out of the pockets of wealthy patrons.

Warner Jones (above, on left), with a young Will Farish and the author, had a fondness for unusual pranks. John M.S. Finney (on the right) led the Fasig-Tipton auctions for many years with a style all his own.

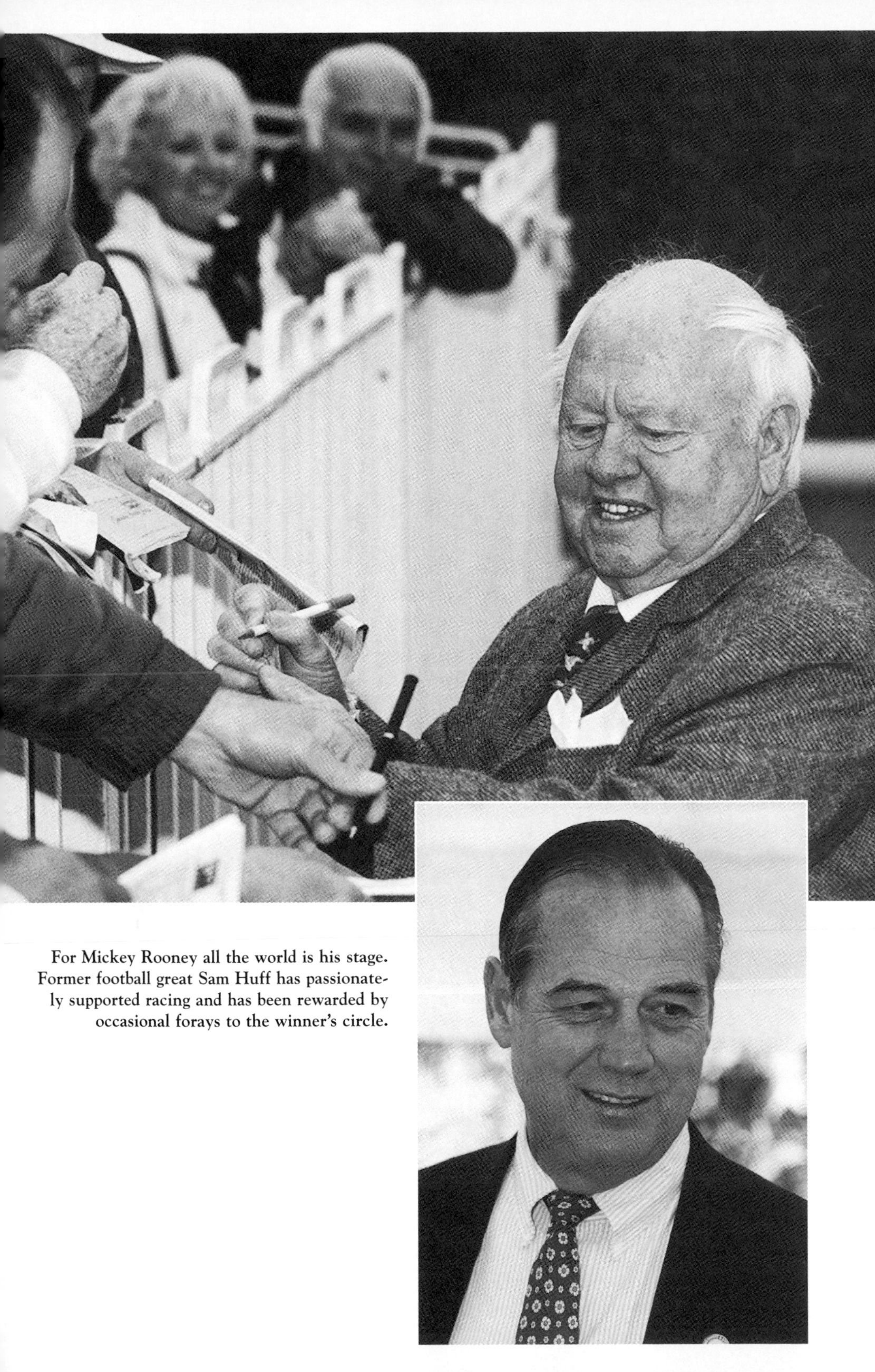

For Mickey Rooney all the world is his stage. Former football great Sam Huff has passionately supported racing and has been rewarded by occasional forays to the winner's circle.

The idiosyncratic Lester Piggott is considered one of the greatest jockeys of all time.

The author thought he had nearly done it all. Then he jumped from an airplane.

Anne Campbell has gone along for the ride with unfailing good humor and support.

warmth and good fellowship, oozing charm from every pore, I stuck out my right hand for a firm handshake, and my left hand swept up to remove my hat. My fingers reached for the crown of my fedora, and as they met only thin air, it dawned on me that I was wearing my *cap*.

Now I was faced with a dilemma that would challenge my savoir-faire. What logical, graceful move could I now make with my left hand hovering over my head? Well, I completely lost my composure. I simply placed my left hand on top of my head, as if this were some sort of ritual of friendship that only I understood.

Having placed it on top of my head, inexplicably I elected to keep it there during the entire social exchange! Thank the Lord this was of a rather short duration.

After a few moments, during which these people stared at me incredulously, I retreated. Only then did I remove my hand from atop my head.

Some minutes later, I saw the gentleman's wife peering anxiously at me across the paddock as if she were observing the troubled antics of an escaped lunatic.

It was not my finest hour.

A Japanese Good-bye

The language barrier has scuttled many a promising business transaction. Here's how the misinterpretation of one single three-letter word frustrated the chances of a major horse transaction in France some years back.

In the early eighties the Japanese entered the horse business with much gusto. Fueled by a strong yen and a booming economy, Japanese horsemen went on serious international shopping sprees. Owners, trainers, and bloodstock agents with horses to sell were drooling over these Japanese visitors.

Their custom has always been to go looking at horses in unwieldy groups of up to a dozen people. How they come to a decision I can't imagine, but their system has worked for them.

The eighties was a time when both Japanese tourists and traders were beginning to venture forth into the world on a wide variety of missions. The Japanese are relatively well-mannered and deferential today, but they were even more so then. They were most anxious to be polite, play by the rules, and never overstay their welcomes.

In the early days of this phenomenon, a sizeable group had come to Paris to buy top race fillies for homeland campaigning and subsequent retirement for breeding.

They were being guided and advised by a French bloodstock agent and were touring the stable yards of Chantilly and other training grounds near Paris. The agent had rented a huge van and a driver to accommodate his client group of nine.

The group arrived at the yard of John Fellowes, a prominent English-French trainer who had three nice fillies for their inspection. The agent had contacted Fellowes and arranged for him to show the fillies to the Japanese at 3:30. The agent apologized that he would be arriving a few minutes late. He was going ahead in his own vehicle to set up the next stable visit. He would return to Fellowes' yard before they were finished, in time to facilitate any discussions and negotiations.

However, Fellowes was not informed that the visitors did not speak a word of French and knew only a few English words.

English and French trainers sell many more horses out of their racing stables than do American trainers, and they present them for purchase with panache.

If you go to Belmont Park to check out a horse, the trainer is often less than enthusiastic about the intrusion, the groom who drags him out is invariably disgruntled at having his routine disrupted, and the window of opportunity to inspect the horse is short-lived.

Their European counterparts, on the other hand, will

invariably offer coffee and tea, and on most days those visiting the yard are invited to stay for an elegant lunch.

These trainers can talk charmingly about the horses in their care (and knowingly about the ones not in their care). When they show you several horses that might fill your bill, they usually have a particular one, strategically placed, that they plan to sell you.

So it was with Fellowes. This visit represented a fine opportunity to sell a Northern Dancer filly with moderate ability and a big price tag. He planned to move her.

The van driver and the nine Japanese horsemen, sans their tour-director bloodstock agent, wheeled in right on time, disembarked, and assembled themselves on the walking ring and awaited the show. Fellowes chattered away graciously, with the visitors nodding and beaming pleasantly and not understanding a single word. The van driver was simply a van driver with little interest in the nature of the visit.

The first horse was brought out. Fellowes said, "Here is a very smart four-year-old filly by the splendid miler, Habitat. She broke her maiden at the tail end of last season and should show much improvement this year, especially at seven to nine furlongs. She acts on any ground and is a very pleasant ride."

The Japanese swarmed around her, as they are prone to do. They took numerous photographs and nodded and smiled a great deal. Fellowes then detected that the examination was over and signaled the lad to put her up.

Next came a gray three-year-old filly. "This attractive filly is sired by the great Mill Reef. She did not start as a two-year-old because of immaturity, but should be poised for a fine year, blah, blah, blah..."

All nine Japanese horsemen again went into their inspection routine, and then the filly was walked away.

Next came the focus of the exercise. A big filly by Northern

Dancer, a sire certain to set the Japanese wild, was brought out and stood up for inspection.

Fellowes picked up the tempo. He was on the muscle now. He was going to sell this filly.

"Here we have an absolutely lovely filly by that marvelous sire, Northern Dancer. I've never had in my possession a three-year-old with more promise. She has shown an extraordinary turn of foot on the gallops at home, and I can hardly wait to start her," the trainer enthused.

The Japanese probably caught the name "Northern Dancer," but otherwise did not grasp a word being uttered.

"The only reason an animal of this magnitude and potential is being offered is due to the complications in the estate which owns her.

"I'm sure you'll agree that nowhere on the continent could you find more quality in a racehorse than in this elegant Northern Dancer filly.

"This filly is a very good buy. (Emphatic now) A good buy… a *good buy*!"

The Japanese now recognized another word they knew: "Good-bye." "Good-bye" meant the party was over. Time to go. Leave.

In an effort to follow protocol, the nine Japanese began smiling, bowing, murmuring "Good-bye" repeatedly, and then disappeared quickly into the nearby van.

In short order, while the stunned Fellowes and his filly watched, the Japanese delegation was gone, heading out to the next stop.

9

Trainer Tales

I am tired of reading, hearing, and thinking about the business of racing. There was a time when you picked up the *Daily Racing Form* or *The Blood-Horse* and read about racehorses, what they had been doing or were about to do — about racing. Now we are besieged with racing politics, chemistry, technical psychobabble, legal maneuverings, governmental machinations, internecine warfare, and a variety of other dreary (but necessary, I am sure!) topics that seem far removed from the wonderful sport of horses trying to outrun one another.

That other stuff is not fun.

This book is meant to be. This chapter is about some of the delightful characters on the training side of horse racing and the wackiness they engendered and encountered.

Jimmy Jones

You had to love Jimmy Jones. Like a baby who first stares at you vacantly and then explodes joyfully into a crinkly-eyed, big smile, so did Jimmy Jones engage you. In the first seconds of contact, he seemed at the same time slightly worried, a tad solicitous, a trifle wary, but searching hard for a reason to smile.

He was one of the "the Jones Boys," one of the greatest horse-training teams in the history of the game. The father was Ben "B.A." Jones, a big, beefy, gimlet-eyed man who brooked no affronts and earned a reputation for being a first-class Midwestern saloon brawler.

Jimmy, on the other hand, was a good-natured, roly-poly little fellow who exuded what appeared to be a childlike innocence. He seemed intent on achieving the most pleasant possible social intercourse with his fellow man, with a voice that was sifted through gravel and a mind like a steel trap!

The Jones Boys came out of Parnell, Missouri, and despite the substantial and inevitable degree of sophistication that must have come simply from the glitter and glamour of winning eight Kentucky Derbys, they remained "Parnell" to the core. The boys left the country, but the country never left the boys.

They made their indelible mark when they signed on as private trainers for the vaunted Calumet Farm, and they quickly set about creating a dynasty that has never been equaled. Their names are associated with the creation of such racing luminaries as Citation, Coaltown, Ponder, Hill Gail, Pensive, Bardstown, Whirlaway, Armed, Bewitch, Tim Tam, Two Lea, Barbizon, Iron Liege, Wistful, On-and-On, A Gleam, etc., etc.

Never has any other horse-training feat equaled the skein of great horses turned out for Calumet by the Jones Boys.

Much of the year they operated in two divisions. In 1948 Jimmy had the Florida division that included Citation (a horse who would make anyone's top-five-horses-of-all-time list). Jimmy actually trained the horse, but when he brought him to Kentucky for the Derby, he had to turn Citation over to his father, who was seeking to tie the record of Derby Dick Thompson, with four victories in that classic. Being a good son — with little choice in the matter! — Jimmy was good-natured about it. But in his later years his bitterness at this injustice surfaced, and he was rather outspoken about it.

I loved Jimmy's recount of bringing the mighty Citation to Louisville: "Coaltown was my father's horse. He had Coaltown in Louisville while I had Citation in Hialeah. When I come up to Louisville with Citation, some of them boys from Louisville started kiddin' me, sayin', 'What you doin' here?' I told them, 'I come over to win the Derby.' They said, 'You won't see anything but a big brown hiney (Coaltown's); that's all you'll see.' I said, 'If he beats this horse, you just call me imbecile for the rest of my life.' "

But my story has to do with an earlier time, the early 1930s in Chicago.

The boys were training for Herbert Woolf out of Kansas City. They had good, solid stock (they were a few years away from winning their first Derby with Lawrin), and they were having a dandy meeting at Arlington Park.

One steaming hot July day Jimmy and Ben were driving down State Street in Chicago's "Loop." Jimmy was behind the wheel, chattering away, while Ben stared stonily ahead.

A big black Packard touring car with four male occupants pulled alongside. The thuggish-looking fellow in the front gestured unmistakably toward the curb, and the Joneses pulled over.

"What the hell!" said Jimmy.

A big, swarthy individual emerged from the back seat and sauntered over to the modest Jones vehicle. He had on black pants, a bow-tie, a white shirt with the sleeves rolled up, and a sailor straw boater.

Jimmy had the sickening feeling that this man looked quite familiar.

The big fellow put a foot on the running board, leaned into the car, and asked, "Which one of youse is the horse trainer...Jones?"

Jimmy piped up, "Why, we both are! I'm Jimmy Jones, and this here is B.A. What can we do for you?"

"Well, my name is Al Capone. You heard of me?"

Two quick affirmative nods.

"I like the races, make a bet or two. Every time I go out to Arlington you guys seem to be winning all the races. You must be good trainers," Capone said.

Now these were pleasing sentiments for the big gangster to be expressing, but somehow neither Jimmy nor Ben sensed that beneficial news would follow.

"I wanna cash a few bets, so I might want to hook up with youse. You probably got a live horse or two left in the barn. Maybe we could have some fun together, and I'll take care of you if we do," Al continued.

Jimmy and Ben deduced that if the "live horse" did not generate fun, indeed they might be taken care of in another way.

Before they could respond, Al Capone issued an invitation. "You come have dinner with me. We'll work it out. Tomorrow night at seven at the Cicero Grill, down on Division Street. Unnastand?"

Capone grinned, nodded abruptly, slapped Jimmy on the shoulder, and strolled back to his car.

"Oh, shit," Jimmy looked at his father. "What're we gonna do now?"

"Hell, we're going to dinner," Ben replied.

The next night the two horse trainers arrived at the Cicero Grill, an establishment of rather modest appointments. There were very few patrons, but the bartender seemed aware they had not just wandered in off the street for a drink. He greeted them with, "Jones? Go through that door next to the kitchen."

They did. They were the first arrivals — save one — in a small private dining room, with a large table with places set for eight. The only other occupant was a forlorn-looking man in a seedy tuxedo. He was clutching a violin.

"What's happening?" Jimmy brightly sought to break the ice (and perhaps learn something about the nature of the evening ahead). The violinist shrugged unhappily and said nothing.

After about fifteen minutes, a mild commotion sounded in the main dining area of the Cicero Grill. The door burst open, and in came Big Al, four of his staff, and, quite surprisingly, a very rotund male child of about eight years. He wore tight short pants. He bore a strong resemblance to Al and was introduced as "my boy, Sonny."

With much backslapping and playful punches, Al Capone jovially launched the social hour. Soon a surprisingly large number of waiters for an establishment the size of the Cicero Grill were hurrying in with drinks and antipasto for this strange assortment of dinner guests: Capone and staff, two nervous horse trainers, a violinist, and a fat little boy.

Jimmy and Ben had, of course, discussed exhaustively what to do about Big Al's keen interest in their racing stock. They had determined it was a no-win situation. If they complied with Al's demand to cut him in on a juicy gambling opportunity, the best-case scenario would be a nice "tip" if the horse won. However, victory was sure to be followed by a request for another such opportunity, and on and on, ad infinitum.

There was considerable downside risk. If the horse did not win, and Big Al dropped a bundle, the relationship would sour significantly, and who knew what ramifications such a failure might wreak.

It did not take a genius to figure out that the boys were up the well-known creek and did not have a paddle.

Their game plan was to agree vaguely to everything and then hope fate would somehow intervene before the moment of truth. Perhaps some strategic stalling would temper Al's enthusiasm for a gamble of this nature.

The business portion of this night's meeting took place during the consumption of the antipasto, with Al's promise that "some high-class entertainment" would follow. Surely this would not be the violinist?

The "business" consisted of, "Now you boys know how to win races. So next time you got something good, you call me and I'll load up with the bookmakers. Unnastand what I'm saying?"

Jimmy and Ben indicated that they did understand.

With that, a very heavy meal commenced, with Al and his boys — and the fat child — laying down a blistering pace and admirable staying power. During dinner Al had signaled Lenny the violinist to favor the group with some renditions, and the musician began sawing away dolorously with a variety of sentimental selections.

In telling the story in later life, Jimmy remembered the room had no windows, and because air conditioning was rare in those days, the single, oscillating electric fan was badly overmatched by the hot Chicago weather. The wine, lasagna, temperature, and the nature of their predicament were combining to make the nervous Jones Boys perspire heavily. If they had been racehorses, they would surely have left their races in the paddock.

The meal finally ended. Thank God, thought the guests; now this dreaded evening must soon be over.

At this point Al belched loudly, scratched his stomach, reared back in his chair, and said, "Now youse are in for a treat. Sonny has been taking singin' and dancin' lessons; I want him to show you his stuff!"

Al's boys signaled the waiters to clear the table, and the guests — Jimmy and Ben — were told to move their chairs back so they could better appreciate the visual nuances of Sonny's presentation, which would take place on top of the dinner table.

Sonny did not suffer from stage fright. With a boost from one of the adults, he scrambled enthusiastically on top of the sturdy table.

Lenny and Sonny had obviously "worked" together, and it

was with seasoned teamwork that the two embarked on "It's Only a Shanty in Old Shantytown." This old favorite brought so much applause that it was followed with the popular "Ma, He's Makin' Eyes at Me." There was a thunderous response in the private dining room, and the Jones Boys carried their share of the load. After five or six other numbers, during which Sonny had managed to break a major-league sweat (and so had the two honored guests), Big Al jumped up and said — Jolson style — "You ain't seen nothin' yet! Now, Angel, show 'em the Lindy Hop and the Charleston." Lenny was beginning to falter slightly, but not Sonny. This was his (and Al's) big moment, and by God he was going to deliver the goods.

The entire Cicero Grill was reverberating until about 10:30, when Al mercifully declared it was time to put "my singin' and dancin' angel to bed." The party — surely the longest night in the lives of Jimmy and Ben Jones — was deemed to be over. Goodnights were said with firm reminders to the two horsemen that Al Capone would be awaiting their call with good news of the upcoming score.

Day after day the Jones Boys played their waiting game, hoping the problem would disappear. A week passed, and they began to have high hopes that Al's lust for a score had been diverted. Then, the dreaded call. "You boys ain't forgot about our project, have ya?" Al had not.

"Uh, no, we're working on it. But the situation has got to be just right. We'll be in touch," Jimmy explained.

"Be in touch before the week's over!" Al suggested.

The boys had a solid three-year-old filly named Missouri Waltz. She was worth about $10,000 in those Depression days, which made her a pretty good horse. The two trainers owned her themselves. So they decided that Missouri Waltz would be the vehicle that would activate the project. They would run this nice filly in a five-thousand-dollar claimer. Missouri Waltz should win easily. Of course, she would surely be claimed (bought), and though that thought was abhorrent, the alternative was more abhorrent.

They found a race six days away, phoned Big Al, and informed him of the play. Capone was very pleased. This must have been a dull period in gangland activities in the Windy City, for the big fellow seemed inordinately interested in what should have been a "small-potatoes" undertaking. There were several subsequent conversations before the big day.

Race day came, and the betting public found it so strange that the canny Jones Boys would drop this filly so drastically that they laid off her, and she went off at 7-2. She should have been 1-5!

Jimmy and Ben were sweating bullets and not terribly enthused about watching the race with Big Al in his box, about which he was most insistent.

But they did, and agonizing though it was, Missouri Waltz waltzed home by five lengths and paid $9.40. Another good fortune for the horse's owners was that other horsemen either shared the bettors' suspicion or noticed Capone's involvement and were afraid to claim a filly that afforded one of the juiciest opportunities of the Chicago summer racing season.

Capone had done most of his betting with bookmakers around the country. He had done well, but more importantly he looked and felt like a genius.

Big Al was most complimentary to Ben and Jimmy Jones. "I knew you guys were good. You done fine! I tellya what — you come on over to the Cicero Grill on Saturday night, and we'll put on the feed bag again. We'll get Sonny to put on another show for us, huh? And we'll talk about where we're going from here! We're going to have some fun this summer! And I'll have an envelope for youse."

Jimmy and Ben went back to the barn. While the filly was cooling out, Ben, leaning pensively against the railing in the shed row, called Jimmy over. "By God, I'll tell you where we're going from here. Soon as there's an eastbound train, and it'd better be a night train, we're taking the whole damned outfit to Latonia. We got to quit while the quittin's good. I don't want no more of this, I don't want the envelope, and I sure to God can't stand another evening with that little fat boy!"

The Jones Boys came back to Chicago, cutting a wide swath when they did. But it was at a time when Big Al was residing in a large concrete structure in Atlanta, as the guest of the federal government.

Buddy Raines (and Whistling Bob)

Virgil W. "Buddy" Raines was the consummate horseman, a wonderful human being, and one of the most uncomplicated, evenly balanced persons God ever let live.

He botched a splendid opportunity to be neurotic. You see, no one ever told him he had a right to be.

Buddy was one of seven children in a poor family. One day an itinerant horse trainer was traveling through Wayne, Illinois, and, in keeping with the neighborliness of the times, was invited to have a meal with the Raines family.

At supper he looked around the table, admired the young manpower sitting there, and said, "Man, I wish I had me a strong little boy to help out with my horses!"

Mr. Raines, keenly cognizant of having an excess number of mouths to feed in times that were hard, said, "Well, hell, take that one," pointing unmistakably at Buddy.

He did, putting Buddy straight to work in what would be the beginning of eighty years in the horse business. After several years as virtually an indentured child servant, Buddy was traded to another horseman. That fellow kept him, worked him, and then "gave" him to a man who was to play a significant part in the boy's development.

This was Whistling Bob Smith, who at that time was the trainer of the powerful Brookmeade Stable of Isabel Dodge Sloane.

Buddy primarily galloped horses for him and later began riding races on the flat and over jumps.

Whistling Bob Smith (so called because of a usually sunny disposition) had a wife who was very kind. She liked Buddy and was the first to be concerned that whatever education Buddy had received thus far had come from life on the racetrack. She insisted that Buddy — age sixteen and doing pretty well financially as a jockey apprenticed to the Brookmeade outfit — be enrolled in school. The schooling could be fitted into his daily barn and racetrack responsibilities.

So enroll he did. Trouble was the young man was shaving every day but his educational background was that of a six-year-old. Buddy Raines had to start out with first grade.

Someone once asked him, "Buddy, wasn't that awfully embarrassing to be in class with all those little kids?"

"Hell no! I was the only sumbitch in the first grade that drove a Pierce Arrow to school!"

Buddy was a perfect example of how the worldliness of the racetrack can turn an ignorant person from humble origins into a relative sophisticate.

Buddy socialized as an equal with giants of industry; he traveled abroad with one of his adoring patrons, Donald Ross; columns were written about him by such as the renowned Red Smith; the legendary chairman of the Coca-Cola Co., Robert W. Woodruff, was delighted by him and once named one of his bird dogs "Buddy Raines."

Buddy wore clothes that would have pleased Cary Grant. He never knew a stranger, was easy with any man or woman from the loftiest station in life, had impeccable manners, was an engaging conversationalist, and, most important of all, he was comfortable and happy in his own skin.

His would surely have been a less captivating story had he not been "given" to that horse trainer who stopped for a meal.

Some of Buddy's unpredictable savoir-faire brushed off from Whistling Bob, but certainly not all of it. Mr. Smith had some rather startling gaps in his urbanity. He retained a fierce addiction to *The Lone Ranger*, a popular radio serial of the thirties and forties featuring a phenomenally benevolent masked cowboy and his faithful companion, a steadfast and taciturn Indian named Tonto.

Each day just before 4:30, Whistling Bob would surreptitiously dart into the tack room, shut the door, and then emerge thirty minutes later, flushed with excitement. Bob may have been the oldest member of The Lone Ranger Fan Club, but by no means was his dedication lacking.

All the help knew what he was doing, but they tactfully refrained from discussing this topic with the big boss.

When Brookmeade ran a horse in a stake (which, of course, it frequently did), the late afternoon timing of this featured race unfortunately would conflict with the *Lone Ranger* episode of that day. One surmises that on these occasions, Whistling Bob opted for the paddock and saddling duties and not for his Philco. Perhaps he knew some ten-year-old fellow fan who could re-create that day's adventures for him.

One day Buddy's boss left the shed row and popped into the tack room for his daily fix.

At five o'clock, just as the last strains of "Hi-Yo Silver! — Away!" were dissipating into the ether, Bob threw open the door and yelled in complete disgust, "Who do those jokers think they're kidding!"

"What's the matter, boss?" Buddy rushed up and asked solicitously.

With a wild look in his eye, Bob Smith exclaimed, "This is crazy! Get this: The Lone Ranger is holed up in a canyon. He's in a helluva gunfight with some rustlers. So he sends a smoke signal to Tonto, who has got to be at least a mile away. No more than one minute later that son of a bitch rides up to help! There's no way in the world he could have got there that fast. Man, I don't know what they're trying to pull!"

In addition to *The Lone Ranger*, Whistling Bob also was a devoted backer of his horses. If he had one ready and the odds were right, he would shove the shekels through the windows with both hands.

Once, in later years, when that great outfit had long since won the Kentucky Derby with Cavalcade, the Belmont with High Quest, and Buddy was still assistant trainer, the old trainer was struck down with a grave illness.

Bob lay seemingly comatose in his hospital room. One afternoon during rounds, his doctor entered the room. A family member asked him about Bob's chances.

The doctor, under the impression that Smith was unconscious, walked the visitor over to the corner of the room and answered, "Truthfully, it's about 10-1 against his survival."

The 10-1 registered with Whistling Bob. His eyes popped open, and he rasped, "Say, Doc, that's too good a price to pass up. Just reach in my pants pocket and get out a ten-dollar bill. I'll take that bet for a sawbuck!"

Buddy Raines was, in the words of Red Smith, "an enemy of silence." He had a thousand great stories and he would tell them, like this one:

Bob Smith sent Buddy up to Narragansett Park with five or six bad horses he wanted to sell. Buddy had written on the back of his condition book the prices the boss wanted for these unsuccessful Brookmeade runners — five hundred dollars for this one, one thousand dollars for that one…and ten thousand dollars for one horse in the bunch. This was a little bay colt named Transparent. He had a touch of class about him.

Buddy found stalls for them, and then he put the word out on the backstretch that on Sunday at 10:30 he would be showing, and selling, these horses.

Buddy got a little carried away with this executive assignment and started "putting on the dog."

"On Sunday morning," Buddy related. "I was reared back in a camp chair, smoking a big cigar. I had two or three grooms bringing horses out and walking 'em in a circle, while I told about what they'd done and how well they would fit in at Narragansett. I had all the prices memorized pretty good, I thought," Buddy related.

"Now this little bay, the best horse, comes by, and a fellow says, 'What'll you take for that one, Buddy?' "

This man had the past performances on this particular colt, but Buddy did not. So Buddy took a quick look at his condition book with the prices. He saw the figure "1" with some zeroes behind it but did not count the zeroes correctly. Buddy, having the time of his life, took a big puff on the stogie, cocked his head at the prospective buyer, frowned thoughtfully, pursed his lips, and said, "Oh, hell, I'll let you have that colt for one thousand dollars."

The man wrote out a check and led the colt back to his barn.

That night Buddy called Bob Smith with the results. "I sold 'em all. Even sold that little bay thing, Transparent."

"Good. What'd you get for him?" Mr. Smith asked.

"One thousand dollars!" Buddy replied.

"A thousand? Why, you dumb bastard, I told you *ten thousand*. Look in the condition book." Smith was correct, of course.

"Don't you even think about coming back here, unless you show up with nine thousand more dollars. Or the horse," Smith screamed.

Buddy was distraught because he knew there was no chance of going back with either.

He had about three hundred dollars of his own, so he went to the buyer of Transparent and offered him a quick three-hundred-dollar profit. No dice. The man knew he had taken someone to the cleaners. Now Buddy was stumped, and he was really terrified.

He said later, "Bob Smith would have sure 'nuff skinned me. I was never so scared of a man. I tried to quit him once, and he liked to have beat the life out of me. When the old man died and was laid out, I went to see him. I touched him and he was cold. I made sure of that. I backed off and told my wife, 'That's the first time I been that close to him when I wasn't a-scared.' "

The buyer of Transparent had a groom whose nickname was Washington D.C. This groom knew Buddy and the next morning saw him in the track kitchen. He asked, "Buddy, did that horse you sold us ever have colic?"

Buddy's heart leapt within his breast! "Why, yes, Wash, he's bad to have the colic. Why do you ask?"

"He sure colicked last night. I was up with him, oiled him, walked him, and he ain't no better today."

"He did, huh?" Mr. Raines was beginning to see a ray of sunshine on a bleak horizon.

Wash said, "Doc's over there now working on him. I'm telling you, he might not make it."

"Hmmm…that's a shame, Wash," Buddy commiserated.

Buddy went back to his barn to tend to the stock that had not been picked up; indeed, he hoped that he might have received a somewhat more empathetic message from Whistling Bob. The last conversation had not been encouraging.

He decided to wait a couple of hours before checking on the "progress" of the stricken Transparent.

Later, Buddy strolled over to the new owner's barn. He called out, solicitously, "Wash, how's that colt coming along?"

"Ain't no way that horse is gonna make it," Wash told him. "Doc said there wasn't a chance. He's fixin' to put him down, I'm pretty sure."

Buddy related, "About that time I seen 'em pulling this horse out of the stall. Dead. I went over to pay my respects and sympathize with the man for his sad bereavement…and take a hard look to make sure the right horse was dead. It was Transparent.

"Believe me, he was the best-looking dead horse I ever did see! It wasn't the ideal solution, but it would do! Brookmeade insurance was still in effect! At least I could go home now."

Buddy was a top-notch horse trainer, but it wasn't because of the high-class help he employed. You would have to say he never set the bar very high when hiring staff. I don't guess anyone ever employed grooms with more colorful names.

To name a few, Buddy had Sheets, Buggy Horse Jack, Airplane Jimmy, Bandages, and Quick Quittin' Steve. He could explain most of them.

"Sheets once went to work for a man, and there wasn't any sheets or pillow cases on his bed in an empty stall.

" 'Where's the sheets?' he inquired of the man.

" 'Sheets?' the man asked. 'What's them?'

" 'You know, them white things you put under the blankets.'

"The man just laughed. The next morning when his foreman asked who he wanted to put on a particular horse, he said, 'Just put Sheets up on him.' His name was Sheets from that time on.

"Buggy Horse Jack came from the trotters. Airplane Jimmy was scared by planes in the war, and whenever one came overhead, he'd run for cover. Bandages was a real clumsy guy. He'd carefully roll his bandages, stack 'em in his wall box, and when he'd open the door, they'd all fall on the ground and come unrolled.

"Quick Quittin' Steve would quit any job he didn't like. He was new with us one August at Saratoga. We were stabled at 'Oklahoma.' I was sending some horses down to Delaware Park, and I told Steve to take his trunk and ride down there with 'em in the van. They left about six o'clock, and about two hours later the van driver called me and says:

" 'What happened to that man? He's gone and so is his trunk. And I just now made my first stop!'

"I saw Steve the next morning back in Saratoga, and I asked him how in the hell he got out of the van. He said when the van driver slowed up going out of Oklahoma, about two hundred yards from our barn, he kicked his trunk out and then jumped behind it. He said he got to worrying about whether there was a good kitchen down there. He said the food at Saratoga was mighty good and he wasn't taking chances on no Delaware Park."

Angel Penna

Angel Penna was a son of Argentina, but as a horseman he was international in every sense of the word. Linguistically, he took a crack at three different languages, sometimes simultaneously! He was surely one of the greatest Thoroughbred trainers who ever lived and also one of the most challenging with whom to communicate.

He trained stakes winners Law Court, Montubio, and Southjet (the latter two winning grade Is) for Dogwood and I never did know what the hell he was talking about.

That's an exaggeration because somehow he managed to be a most delightful and expressive companion. He had a marvelous sense of humor, and he was very witty (I think). His face helped immeasurably because it was constantly and eloquently assisting with his dialogue. There were fearsome scowls, moments of beaming exuberance, beatific benevolence, vigorous rolling of the eyes, glances heavenward to invite God's sympathy, weary looks of resignation, and constant shoulder shrugging. All of these were accompanied by guttural grunts and a strange quasi-tap dancing shtick to help sell his point. You eventually got the gist of all this pantomime.

One of our horses, Montubio — once suffered a severe case of colic. The vet was summoned. He oiled him in an effort to unblock the impacted bowel. The treatment was successful, and soon the horse was able to eliminate waste material.

When I called Angel to ascertain the horse's condition, I was delighted to hear the lilt in his voice and to get his down-to-earth report: "Oh, he ees very fine now. He have *many* poo-poo!"

Angel defined the word volatile yet was as kind a fellow as you would ever know. An unforgettable character.

He looked like my idea of a dashing, decidedly upscale gaucho. Angel was of moderate height but had short, bandy legs attached to a torso belonging to a bigger man. He was heavy, not fat, and strong, with very wide shoulders. Penna's face was weathered, with a prominent nose and bright, intelligent eyes. His hair, beginning to thin, looked as if it had been painted on his head.

Penna was a natty dresser. No blue jeans for him. He wore cavalry twill trousers, a smart checked shirt with an ascot or, at least, a colored handkerchief knotted debonairly around his neck. He usually wore a sport coat. His paddock boots were shined daily, by someone in the barn, I would imagine. This was a trainer who would probably be attired in a dark blue business suit when he saddled a horse. He had style galore.

Penna trained in Argentina, Venezuela, France, and America and produced champions in the latter three. He won practically every great race in Europe, including two Prix de l'Arc de Triomphes with the fillies San San and Allez France.

San San's regular rider was Jean Cruguet, but he had been injured five days before the Arc and was replaced by Freddie Head. After winning the race, Angel first went to find Cruguet. He cupped the rider's face in his hands and tearfully commiserated that the sidelined jockey had not been able to experience the thrill of this victory. Never mind that a week earlier Angel might have chased Cruguet out of the stable yard in a towering rage.

Penna won practically every great race in Europe except the English Derby, and many great races in this country but not the Kentucky Derby.

Over here he trained for Ogden Phipps, Gus Ring, Frank Stronach, Dogwood, and Peter Brant among others.

His wife aided him enormously. Elinor Penna served as sort of a conversational facilitator, explaining a little here, cuing Angel at certain times, and defusing when necessary. She was a former sports commentator, a keen student of the racing scene, well-connected socially, and a wit of the first dimension. Angel also had a son, Angel Jr., a first-rate trainer in his own right, to whom he was devoted.

Talking on the phone with Penna was the most difficult form of communication because you were robbed of the visual aids. When "call waiting" was first offered, for some reason Angel, who really did not relish talking on the phone, ordered it on his barn line. This service threw him into a constant tizzy, and he switched in confusion back and forth from one caller to another, often pursuing the wrong subject with the wrong party and usually disconnecting both parties.

Elinor puzzled, "I don't know why he wants to tackle *two* callers. He can't even talk to one person on the phone."

I once gave Angel a gigantic Nijinsky filly to train. Her name was Helenska. He took a long time with her, as he was prone to do. Of course, I wanted to get a line on her, and I periodically sought his opinion.

"What do you think of this filly so far, Angel?" I would ask from time to time.

"Ahhh! Too beeg…too beeg!" he would exclaim, throwing

his arms and head skyward, to seek divine assistance.

The filly bucked her shins finally, and I took her back to the farm to be fired. When she got over this ailment, I decided to send her to another trainer because I was convinced Angel did not like her (Is that not what "too beeg…too beeg" implied?).

She did go to another barn. When Angel recognized her training on the racetrack one morning, he went ballistic. It seems he loved the filly all along, was looking forward to getting her back, and was crushed that I had insulted him by sending her to another man.

He called me up and "fired" me, told me to remove my horses from his barn. Knowing this storm, legitimate though it may have been, would blow over soon, I phoned the next day and was finally able to smooth his ruffled feathers. This was one time when Elinor's interpretive services were badly needed.

He was truly an internationally renowned trainer and had ruled the roost on three continents. He was *the man*! He knew it, and his barn knew it. It was run with the precision of West Point. His staff adored him, struggled to please him, and treated him like a king.

He was at his barn fourteen to sixteen hours a day. When the Allen Jerkenses and the Pennas went out to dinner, four cars were necessary. Both Elizabeth Jerkens and Elinor Penna knew that Allen and Angel would be going back to the barn for an hour or two after dinner.

Amazingly, Penna could get a horse ready to run a mile and a quarter — and win — first time out. Inexplicably, he never seemed to breeze the horse. He had what he called "happy gallops," which were just that: exuberant, open gallops that lasted maybe a half-mile, but more likely a quarter-mile. There was nothing noteworthy or detectable in his training regimen that would explain this singular magic. And you sure as hell couldn't ask him. He might take a long time to get a horse ready to run, but when his horses were led to the paddock, they were ready to crack. His horses were happy and they were fit, or they weren't put in the entries.

He liked to ride Vasquez, Bailey, and Cruguet, and he loved Angel Cordero, who had a flair for kidding him into a jolly frame of mind. But one time Cordero could not.

Penna had brought to this country a very good horse named Lyphard's Wish. The colt was ready for his first race, and Angel Cordero would be riding him.

Penna was not noted for his precise riding instructions, but he knew exactly what he wanted. According to Cordero, Penna's instructions were something like, "Don't take no hold. If they walk, you walk. If they go fast, you walk. When you get there…you move!" If this is verbatim, one can understand the jockey's confusion (although Cordero never paid any attention to instructions anyway!). Cordero swore that Penna always instructed to "move when you get there." But he never said where "there" was!

This day Lyphard's Wish, fresh and running for the first time in strange surroundings, roared out of the gate, hit the front, and ran off with Cordero. At the sixteenth pole, the rank horse was out of gas and got beat, thoroughly embarrassing Cordero and infuriating Penna in the process.

When the rider dismounted and weighed in, there was Angel Penna doing his little jig of rage. The veins in his neck were distended, he was flinging his arms about, and his visage was wreathed in wrath.

There's an old, inexplicable racetrack expression concerning a horrible riding effort: "You rode like a Chinaman!"

This expression had subliminally found earlier residence in Penna's head. He sputtered for words powerful enough to express his utter contempt for Cordero's ride.

"What you do? What you do? You ride thees horse like a uh, uh, black man!" The Puerto Rican Cordero replied, as he walked with the trainer back toward the jockey's room, "Well, hell, I am a black man. What do you think these are — blonde curls?"

Angel Cordero thought it was funny. So did Angel Penna — about two days later.

Doug Davis

The nicest compliment I ever received came from big, blustery Doug Davis, a horseman's horse trainer.

Perhaps the nature of the compliment will indicate that I have been pitifully desperate for kind words. But I loved it.

In my early years in the horse business, I found it quite expedient to buy horses on terms. Oversimplified, this means I bought the horse by paying one-third of the purchase price down, took possession of the animal, and deferred the balance over two payments six months apart. This was unheard of in this industry when I first started doing it. I could do it because I had earned a good reputation. Any deviations from the payment schedule would be in favor of the seller. I saw to that.

One year in a horses-of-all-ages paddock sale at Saratoga, Doug Davis was selling (on behalf of his major patron) a good race filly named Jill the Terrible. She figured to be pricey, but I wanted to buy her. Before the sale I asked the owner, whom I knew only slightly, if he would provide me with terms if I were the successful bidder. He was a little skittish about this, hemmed and hawed, and said he'd have to think it over and get back to me.

Later that day, this fellow walked up to me and said, "I asked Doug Davis if he thought I would be safe in selling that filly to you on terms. Doug told me, 'Well, I just wish that son of a bitch owed me a quarter of a million dollars!' "

From that day on, I've had a warm spot in my heart for Doug Davis.

Doug had style, presence, and charisma. When he walked into a room, you knew he was there. He made any gathering more interesting. He was a big man with a thunderous voice and a gaudy appetite for life.

As a child he must have been influenced by Tom Mix or Hopalong Cassidy because he went "western" all his life. When he died, his estate included seventy-five pairs of cowboy boots and sixty cowboy hats.

Until Wayne Lukas wrested the title away, Doug Davis was the winningest trainer in Keeneland history. This was accomplished when Keeneland certainly offered fine racing, but was not as stylish as it is today. Doug was predominantly a "Midwestern" trainer. He seldom ventured to big-time tracks in New York, Florida, or California. He had mostly Grade B stock, much of which he bred from Hempen, a stallion owned by Davis and known for throwing speed and precocity.

But Doug trained many stakes winners, one of which went to Saratoga and jerked a knot in the best of the Eastern stock in the prestigious Travers Stakes. This was Annihilate 'em, "faster than the word of God" and able to carry that speed over a distance.

When the colt got good, Doug loaded him up in a gooseneck trailer, threw in Charlie, his famous and remarkable stable pony, and a few more runners, and headed up to the Spa.

This entourage created a bit of a reaction at Saratoga. In the first place, gooseneck trailers were not *de rigueur* at Saratoga. Doug himself went over with "the Establishment" like a bastard at a family reunion, and, on top of that, he had a stable pony that functioned without a bridle!

I must admit, the first time I ever saw Charlie smoothly shepherding a jittery runner to the post, I was flabbergasted. Charlie was equipped with not one bit of leather from his shoulders forward and depended entirely on his own incredible savvy and an occasional bit of knee or heel pressure (or mental telepathy!) from the rider.

The Saratoga outriders and stewards were aghast when Doug came on the track the first morning. Astride the seemingly nonchalant and bridleless Charlie, the old Kentucky boy was taking Annihilate 'em out for a gallop several days before the Travers.

An outrider came loping up to this strange little group and said, "You'll have to get that pony off this racetrack. He hasn't got a bridle on!"

Doug explained, "Aww, I know, but he's fine. Charlie don't like anything around his head." He thought that would take care of the intrusion.

"Off! Right now! We're not going to have lead ponies out here with no bridles on them. We've got the safety of the racetrack to consider. Go borrow another lead pony," the outrider firmly ordered.

Doug was not one to duck a confrontation. He shot back, "Well, this lead pony has forgot more about racetrack procedure than all the damned outriders and stewards in New York state will ever know. If this pony goes, I go, and so does this horse that come here to run in the Travers." Doug turned his caravan and headed back to the barn.

He was loading the gooseneck a few minutes later when up hustled a steward and said that they had decided to make a dispensation. Charlie (without a bridle, of course) could escort Annihilate 'em on the racetrack and to the post for the Travers.

The press had a field day with this brouhaha.

About five o'clock three days later the odd couple, Annihilate 'em and Charlie, were the featured attraction in the post parade. Every eye was glued on them.

Annihilate 'em easily won the 1973 Travers, but it was almost anticlimactic to the post parade featuring the Kentucky horse's bridleless escort. The colt's victory finished off properly one of the most colorful chapters in the history of that fine race.

Saratoga lore will always maintain a prominent spot for Annihilate 'em. And Doug Davis. And for Charlie — just a working guy who "didn't like anything around his head."

While he was for many years the winningest trainer at Keeneland, one year, despite running two or three horses every day, Davis did not win a single race.

In racing, a "duck" (yes, a fowl!) is presented to the trainer who finishes the meeting without a single winner to his name. I don't know the reason for this custom. But there is always a lot of chortling around the racing secretary's office about whether so-and-so (ideally a high-profile trainer!) "is going to get the duck."

This particular year Doug had slightly aroused the ire of his good friend and longtime training competitor, Herb Stevens — a crusty citizen and a bona fide character in his own right.

Early in this Keeneland meet, Herb had entered a first-time starter in a maiden claiming race. Much to Herb's surprise, Doug claimed him. While this action did not enrage Herb, it did get his attention. After the race, when the horse was ensconced in his new barn, Doug came running over to his pal Herb and said, "Herb, I couldn't help it. This damned owner of mine out in Arkansas made me claim that horse. I didn't want to."

Herb said later, "I didn't care about losing the horse, but it made me mad as hell that Davis would think I was dumb enough to believe that cock-and-bull story."

On closing day at Keeneland, Doug had three runners. The

first two ran in early races and failed to hit the board, and now he had one last chance, in the last race.

Herb Stevens had, of course, been keeping tabs on the big guy, and he was not pulling for Doug to mar his winless record by knocking off the tenth and last race.

About mid-afternoon Herb strolled into the secretary's office. The staff had purchased and put on display a life-sized, lawn ornament-type duck, to be presented to Davis, if he kept his dismal record unscathed in the last race.

Herb said, "Give me that damned duck! I'm gonna make *this* presentation."

He then alerted the press box, the track photographer, and anyone else he could think of to be in the Keeneland walking ring for a very meaningful ceremony. He arranged for several other fellow trainers — individuals who would tend to enjoy the nature of the project — to grab Davis after the last race (if indeed, he did not win it) and escort him to the ceremonial site.

The training fraternity got the exact result it desired: Doug's horse did not even threaten. So Doug was steered, almost forcefully, back to the walking ring.

There, gleefully assembled were every racing writer in central Kentucky, a variety of photographers, most of the staff of Keeneland, and a sizeable group of curious racing fans now exiting the track past the walking ring. It was a splendid crowd, and in the middle of it was Herb Stevens with the duck — on a leash!

Accompanied by lusty jeering, Stevens dealt thoroughly with Davis' lack of accomplishment at this Keeneland meeting, made the presentation, and concluded with, "Now, Doug, this makes us even!"

A resulting photograph of Doug, staring balefully down at the duck he held on a leash and clearly at a very unaccustomed loss for words, is a classic. It still hangs on the walls of several racing secretary offices and press boxes at tracks where Doug Davis plied his trade.

It may have been the only duck Doug Davis ever received.

10

Nothing Happens Until . . .

Hanging on the walls of half the salesmen in America is the slogan, "Nothing Happens Until Somebody Sells Something!" If you're in the Thoroughbred horse business, this should be changed to "Everything Happens When Somebody Sells Something (or tries to)!"

The racing of Thoroughbred horses is a thrilling, fascinating, colorful, and risky undertaking. But, know this: the *selling* of those Thoroughbred horses is equally thrilling, fascinating, colorful, and risky.

Some of our greatest characters have devoted themselves to that side of the game. They all loved racing and were hooked by it, but providing the ammunition is what they were all about.

Here we deal with three of the most flamboyant.

Leslie Combs

You've heard of people who "broke the mold." Well, "Cousin" Leslie Combs is one of them.

In his day, if he wasn't king of the horse business, he was in strong contention; and he was under the impression that he already owned that title.

He would tell you he was going to sell you a horse, you were going to pay through the nose for it, and you were going to have the time of your life in the process. And then he would deliver the goods. He bred and sold some wonderful horses.

I bought some horses from his Spendthrift Farm through the years, but I am a bargain buyer and, therefore, just a tiny blip on his radar screen. He didn't expend much of his legendary charm on me. He didn't want to run me off, but peewees like me were slim pickings for a salesman like Leslie who had two rows of seats in the Keeneland sales pavilion warmed by the affluent derrieres of such as Dolly Green, Art and Martha Appleton, Frank McMahon, Franklin Groves, John Olin, Martha Kilroe, Elizabeth Arden Graham, and John W. Hanes.

Woody Stephens, the legendary trainer, used to say, "If you want to be a big flea, you gotta get on a big dog!"

Believe me, that was the battle cry of Leslie Combs.

Monday night at Keeneland was Combs Night, and Spendthrift might be selling as many as eighteen yearlings. You can bet Cousin Leslie had planned painstakingly and struggled tirelessly to orchestrate the successful sale of each.

And could he get the job done! He reigned for fifteen consecutive years as Keeneland's top consignor and held the title three other years.

Ryan Mahan, now head auctioneer at Keeneland, tells a typical Combs story. It took place when Mahan was a young bid spotter (assigned to Combs' section) on the July night the maestro was selling a Northern Dancer colt, a half brother to the great Mr. Prospector.

When the clock struck eight that night and the auction staff began its announcements before the first horse was led in the ring, Combs and his guests were already well ensconced in their seats. The host had seen to it that the cocktail hour at the big house had started early enough for all guests to become sufficiently relaxed, and then he had hustled them into limousines so that the motorcade to Keeneland could get started at 7:30. This was a night for punctuality!

Leslie had long since decided that one of his perennial sales-time guests, Dolly Green, who had been left half the real estate of downtown Los Angeles, should be favored with ownership of the beautifully bred colt that was the star of his consignment.

Interestingly, Keeneland was concerned about including the colt in its "select" sale. His front-end alignment was somewhat askew. As the Irish say, one leg went to Limerick and the other to County Cork! But Keeneland had been assured by Leslie that he had him sold and that the colt would bring one million dollars or more. Naturally, they took him.

Arriving at the pavilion, the Spendthrift aggregation settled in the two rows of seats, with much last-minute stage direction from Cousin Leslie. The seating had to be finely tuned so that no heavy hitters were left unattended out in left field.

Leslie had situated himself next to Dolly Green, you may be sure.

The big colt (for promotional purposes Combs referred to him as "Pretty Boy") was due to sell about 9:15, and Leslie's severe challenge was to see that Mrs. Green did not become bored during the hour and fifteen minutes she would be required to wait. In the interim Leslie had other important horses to sell, and he wanted to "can *all* the fruit" before and after Mrs. Green's anticipated featured transaction.

The sale started. Spendthrift sold a filly and a colt early in the sale. Everything was humming along satisfactorily. But about 8:20 Dolly Green turned to Leslie and complained, "Leslie, I'm cold!"

"Yes, Dolly, Keeneland does keep it too cold in here. I've told 'em about that! You just cuddle up next to Cousin Leslie," Combs leered.

Feeling the need for some stimulus for the pending task, Leslie called out to Ryan Mahan, tuxedo-bedecked and spotting bids in the aisle ten feet away. "Hey there, Mr. Bid Spotter, my 'Pretty Boy' (the Mr. Prospector half brother) is gonna be in here in a few minutes, and you'll see the pretty boy that is going to win the Kentucky Derby!" He squeezed Dolly's arm delightedly. Ryan, fully cognizant of the drill, smiled responsively and nodded vigorously.

Ten minutes went by, and Dolly's attention span was in serious trouble. "Leslie, I'm freezing! It's *uncomfortable* in here."

"It certainly is, Dolly." (Aside to the spotter: "Let's turn that damned thermostat up a little, son!")

"Here, darlin', take Cousin Leslie's coat. If all these people weren't in here, the two of us would do some snuggling. I'd get you warm!" He cackled charmingly and gallantly draped his blue blazer around Dolly's bare shoulders. He sent his son into the bar for a cup of hot coffee laced with a shot of brandy.

It was now twenty-five long minutes away from the appearance of Hip Number 101, for Leslie the focal point of the evening...the *year*! Could Dolly last? It was going to be close.

At 9:05 Dolly rose to her feet. "Leslie, I simply must leave. I am most uncomfortable!"

Leslie, on his feet now, screaming at Ryan and putting on a show for Dolly: "Goddamn it, boy, get Bill Greely (Keeneland general manager). I want this temperature fixed. This lady is cold! And my 'Pretty Boy' is fixin' to come in here, and we want to see him."

Ryan nodded worriedly, and before another horse came into the ring, he hightailed over to the thermostat and pretended to fiddle with it. He then gave the high sign to Combs that everything was corrected. Trying to help, Ryan leaned in to Dolly Green and assured her, "Ma'am, we've warmed it up. You'll be comfortable now!"

This ploy was good for ten minutes. Now the colt was in the ring.

Combs had his coat on Dolly, his arm draped around her, and was practically sitting in her lap. She was drinking her hot coffee, and at last she seemed somewhat interested in the proceedings.

Hip Number 101 opened at $300,000, then jumped to $400,000. The reserve had been reached, and now any bids would be live ones.

Leslie turned and smiled expectantly at Dolly. She nodded vaguely, and Ryan bellowed, "Yep!!!" The colt went to $500,000.

Combs might have signaled to someone in the pavilion. The bid jumped to $600,000.

At that point the great showman leaned forward in his seat, waved idiotically at the colt in the ring and sang out, "Hello there, 'Pretty Boy.' You gonna win that Derby for Leslie and Dolly aren't you, 'Pretty Boy'?"

Dolly whispered impatiently to Leslie that she wanted to bid again. Leslie's hand on her shoulder fluttered for $700,000.

Mysteriously, the bid kept jumping on past a million, until Dolly bid a cool million two hundred.

At that point Dolly stood up and said, "Oh, Leslie, I just can't bid anymore." It was her bid. She didn't have to.

With his arm around her, they were starting up the aisle. Surprisingly, they heard "One million, three hundred thousand." Leslie couldn't believe it. But with the guts of a bandit, he whispered, "You might just want to try one more bid, darlin'. Shall we do just one more on our 'Pretty Boy'?"

In exasperation she said, "Oh, I suppose so, but then do let's go."

Leslie Combs, looking back over his shoulder and never breaking stride, unabashedly but emphatically waved in another bid — for $1,400,000. Sold!

The twosome disappeared out the door, and Leslie Combs deposited her into the warmth of the waiting limousine.

Dolly had some nice horses through the years, but this one was certainly not a standout. His name was Yukon. He never won. He never even raced. With that pedigree, he did go to stud but did not emulate either his daddy or his half brother.

Warner Jones Revisited

"Hahhhd dam, Buddy!"

That was his war cry. In a gruff, gravelly voice that rumbled like a freight train barreling over a trestle, that which followed from Warner L. Jones was sure to be either interesting, valuable, or funny...and much of the time outrageous.

We dealt with this Louisvillian in the chapter on "Drinkers and Drinking." He ceased to provide material for that category about thirty years before he died in 1994. He joined Alcoholics Anonymous back then and never took another drink. He cut a wide swath before and a wider, more important swath afterward. He accomplished much in both eras, but certainly an incredible amount in his sober years.

A tribute to his charisma and charm was that many, many people thought they were Warner's best friend. He had several hundred best friends, and I was one. One reason I qualified was that my early years were similarly tumultuous by my own doing.

He liked for me to help him on his reserves at sales, meaning that he got me to bid on his horses to see that they got to the right "neighborhood." One noteworthy example involved the highest-priced yearling ever sold. This Nijinsky colt out of My Charmer, the dam of Seattle Slew, brought a final bid of $13,100,000. He asked me to bid "up to ten million dollars." I asked no questions and did it, although he didn't need me. I had to hurry just to get the opportunity to raise my hand once during this history-making transaction.

Warner made a lot of money, but he did start with some money. He had a pedigree about like that Nijinsky colt. And he came from a background that would have provided a lot of "advantages."

When he was about ten, he was enrolled in Aiken Preparatory School in South Carolina.

He had never been away from home in his life, and despite

his legendary toughness and outward bravado, he was understandably homesick.

One day, he was staring out his classroom window thinking about home and family, and he was overcome with homesickness (a serious malady, as most of us know). Warner started quietly sobbing. A big day student sitting in front of him turned around to look at Warner, laughed, and began taunting him.

"Ooh, just look at the mama's boy. Him is crying for his mama! Is he homesick for Kentucky?" On and on it went.

When Warner was telling me about this incident, I commiserated with him, "Gosh, that was terrible, Warner! What did you do?"

"Hahhhd dam, buddy. When recess came, I grabbed that big son of a bitch and kicked his ass all over that school yard!!!"

That was Warner Jones: sensitive, but tough.

Warner spent much of the year on entertainment and "sales promotion" designed to assure that when his yearlings went to market they would bring good money.

In the early eighties, the Arab sheikhs were spending millions at yearling sales in this country, creating a feeding frenzy in the horse business. Every consignor dreamed of making strong connections with this bottomless supply of greenbacks. Gaining direct access to the sheikhs themselves, however, was extremely difficult. These mysterious men of Saudi Arabia and the United Arab Emirates had zero interest in social invitations.

But each of the Arab princes had at least one bloodstock adviser. Invariably, these were elderly English horsemen of very refined backgrounds — and sporting military rank designations of captain, major, colonel, with an occasional lord and sir popping up. And these gentlemen *were* susceptible to entertainment.

The huge and sudden manifestation of Arab interest was an unexpected bonanza to these types. They were not overly busy beforehand, I think.

One of the most important was Sir Hubert Courtland (as we'll call him). His connection to one of the most powerful and enthusiastic sheikhs did not escape Warner Jones. While his heart was not really in it, Warner and his wonderfully supportive wife, Harriet, invited Sir Hubert and Lady Marjorie for a week-long visit at their winter home in Delray Beach, Florida.

The English couple accepted and flew over to West Palm Beach, where the Joneses met them. The foursome embarked on what was to be a week of pleasant and varied resort activities, with Warner avoiding any hard sell on the yearling crop going to market in several months.

Once they had settled in, Warner suggested to Sir Hubert that a round of golf at Seminole might be just the ticket after a long, tedious journey across the Atlantic.

"Do you know…I've never had an inclination to take up that game," Sir Hubert told his host.

This was not good news.

"Well then, tomorrow we'll take the girls and go out on the boat. The king mackerel are running now, and we could really have some fun," Warner offered.

"Oh, I'm afraid not," Lady Marjorie jumped in. "Both Hubert and I are horrid sailors. We get queasy as soon as the boat leaves the dock!"

That night after dinner, Harriet suggested the two couples play a few rubbers of bridge.

"Not much for card games. Never saw the good of it," Sir Hubert responded.

So the first day ended with golf, fishing, and bridge having been struck off the list. Still, there is plenty to do in Florida.

The next morning after breakfast, Warner suggested they all drive down to Gulfstream for lunch and racing.

"Oh, really now! This is my vacation to get away from racing," the English guest replied.

Tennis? Didn't play.

Backgammon. Afraid not.

Sunbathing on the beach, swimming, strolling on the sand? Sir Hubert explained, "Marjorie's fair skin simply does not permit it. She would be burned to a crisp in minutes."

Now racing, tennis, aquatic activities, and backgammon were eliminated. What was left? Mud wrestling?

That night the thoroughly discouraged, but dead-game Joneses and Sir Hubert and Lady Marjorie went to the Gulfstream Club for dinner (they did eat!).

An orchestra was playing. Warner gritted his teeth and asked the very rotund Lady Marjorie if she would like to dance, hoping fervently that this activity would also be unacceptable. No such luck. She graciously took his hand and the couple glided out on the floor, Warner looking as if he could bite a tenpenny nail in two.

About halfway around the floor, the host smiled dutifully at his partner. She wriggled excitedly and gushed, "Oooh, Mr. Jones, this is heavenly. I do so love to dance. Dancing is truly my weakness, my greatest pleasure. I could just go on dancing the night away!"

In telling the story later, Warner explained, "Hahhhd dam, buddy! Every time I'd get tired, I'd think about those million-dollar yearlings, and I just kept pushing that old fat gal around the floor."

John M.S. Finney

To me, John M.S. Finney was a man who had never been young...yet he would never be old. He was John Finney; he was there and was always going to be...and thank God for it. So vivid was his personality that it was inconceivable that he would not continue to enliven the Thoroughbred racing scene. But he died in 1994.

Selling Thoroughbreds was his game, and he will always be remembered as the head of Fasig-Tipton. He worked for that fine auction company most of his life and was bred to run it. And run it he did, in his own colorful style, at a time when it was in its heyday. But John was painting with broad strokes indeed, and his grandiose expansion plans collided with the economic reality of the late eighties, and problems arose. He left Fasig-Tipton late in his business life and became a high-level bloodstock agent. He was successful, of course, but his name will always be synonymous with Fasig-Tipton.

The colorful son succeeded a colorful father, the legendary Humphrey Finney. John said he was perceived to be "the second cup of tea from the same bag." He may have been at first, but the second cup proved plenty potent.

Keeneland, Fasig's only real competitor, was solid, sensible, and perhaps almost paternal. Fasig-Tipton was run in what seemed to be a loosey-goosey style by a fun-loving, delightful, but ever-so-effective bunch of characters. On the team along with Finney were Ralph Retler, Laddie Dance, D.G. Van Clief, Walt Robertson, Terence Collier, and Steve Dance, with Tyson Gilpin and Clay Camp not officially on the staff but firmly connected as "house consignors." To say that they were jovial men would be like saying that Frank Sinatra could carry a tune.

Fasig-Tipton was "Robin Hood and his Merry Men" to Keeneland's "King Arthur."

No human being ever enjoyed the good life as much as John Finney. Never had a more impish, rapier-like wit fueled an endless supply of deliciously spicy anecdotes. No man ever possessed such a flair for walking amongst socialite-sportsmen, aristocrats, con artists, and good old boys and keeping them all placated. It almost seemed an incongruity that he combined these characteristics with what was an unswervingly rigid code of ethics.

John's great wit was celebrated. An example came from Snowden Carter, Maryland racing journalist and horseman. Snowden was in Saratoga for the yearling sale, mostly as a spectator, but with his antenna out for any worthwhile business opportunities. Snowden tells of one that did come his way:

"About eight o'clock on opening night, I took a seat in the mezzanine of the Humphrey S. Finney sales pavilion. I had heard announcer John Finney give his spiel thousands of times and sort of prided myself on being able to translate the meaning of his carefully constructed sentences (he never told a lie, but he was ever so clever in avoiding disclosure of faults).

"I watched and listened to the voices of Finney and Laddie Dance, the auctioneer, in something of a Saratoga trance until a colt by First Landing, out of Spanked, by Cornish Prince entered the ring.

"John's sales pitch included a confession. The colt was a ridgeling (only one descended testicle) — a required announcement at all horse sales. Offsetting this downer was the fact that the colt was a sharp-looking individual and his dam was a half sister to Affirmed.

"When the bidding hung at around $25,000, I got agitated. I had bought many horses at Fasig-Tipton auctions in Maryland but never above $5,000.

"John Finney looked at his audience in disbelief. 'Do you realize the potential in this colt's pedigree? Sure he's a ridgeling, but some really top horses are ridgelings. Except for that one thing, this is a really fine colt.'

"I had never seen the colt before he came into the ring. But Finney had. And he said flat-out, unequivocally 'This is a really fine colt.' That was enough for me. I trusted him. Up went my hand. Then there was a bid against me. Another nod from me. I got him for $30,000.

"I signed the slip. Wasn't too upset. Figured something good would happen. Like, for example, the annual yearling sale at Timonium. It was only six weeks away — maybe I could get my colt in that catalog even though the closing date had passed.

"Checked with the Timonium sales office before I went to bed. They said they'd let me know in the morning.

"Restless night, and up early the next morning to see my $30,000 baby.

"Insured him, hired van space, and got him entered in the Maryland auction.

"After attending to those vital details, I walked toward the little coffee counter near the sales pavilion. And who should be coming the other way but John Finney. He said, 'You know, Snowden, I've been thinking about it, and I've come to the conclusion that you and that colt you bought last night have something in common.'

" 'What's that?' I asked eagerly.

"Replied Finney, 'You're both half nuts!' "

When Fasig-Tipton was in its heyday in the mid-eighties, the company generated considerable cash flow. Finney wanted to make hay while the sun was shining and had his eye peeled for expansion opportunities. Some made sense; some did not. One from the latter category was his trip to Georgia to discuss with me the possibility of buying the Dogwood operation. He already knew a lot about us, but that "affinity," as he typically termed it, would not have worked, and we both quickly realized it.

One thing that intrigued Finney was the aforementioned Dogwood concept of buying horses on terms. Terms were old stuff in private transactions, but the idea of doing so with horses sold by consignors at public auction was avant-garde, to put it mildly.

With me, invention was the mother of necessity! Coming from an area where banking connections understood precious little about the Thoroughbred industry, it was difficult in the early days to arrange an adequate line of credit — and this was in an era when horses were selling like expensive hotcakes.

Consequently, I conceived the idea of going to a consignor and saying, in effect, "Look, you know me and Dogwood's reputation. Why then would you not be comfortable with an arrangement where — if I am successful in buying one of your horses (with no pre-arranged price in mind, of course) — you will permit me to pay for that horse over a period of a year."

Spendthrift Farm was the first to go for it. Lee Eaton, the pre-eminent sales agent of the day, embraced the idea, and soon practically every consignor was willing to sell me horses in this manner.

The sales companies liked it fine. They got their full commission out of the first payment. Furthermore, it put another strong bidder in the market (with a little more guts than he might normally have had paying cash). Additionally, though I might not end up with the horse, my presence might have pushed the ultimate buyer a little higher.

An example of John's complete fairness is the fact that Fasig-Tipton had its own financing arm. It was called TECO (Thoroughbred Equity Company), but its arrangement was nowhere near as beneficial to me as the terms I was enjoying. Finney knew this, and still he tried wholeheartedly to sell any reluctant consignor on cooperating with the Dogwood terms "package."

He was smooth as silk, but he had been known to lose his cool.

In 1975 John's pal LeRoy Jolley (another renowned wit), won the Kentucky Derby with Foolish Pleasure.

After the Derby the colt shipped to Baltimore for the Preakness at Pimlico. Foolish Pleasure was going to have a maintenance breeze five days before the race, and LeRoy invited John Finney to come out to Pimlico at 7:00 a.m. when the Foolish Pleasure entourage would leave the barn and head to the racetrack for the breeze. As with all racehorses — and

Triple Crown runners for damn sure — there was no leeway in the timing. He would go at 7:00!

John was delighted, and he invited Terence Collier, a key Fasig-Tipton staffer, to come along. Terence asked if he might bring two visiting equine auction executives from Europe. John said fine. They would all meet in the lobby of the Cross Keys Hotel, where they were staying. The time would be 6:30 a.m. — sharp!

The next morning John and Terence were there, but the two visitors were late. John paced a bit, went and got the car, and pulled it up front. By now it was 6:40, and both he and Terence were fuming. At 6:45 the two men showed up, and off they roared to Pimlico, about ten minutes away. John was quite tense — for him.

They pulled up to the stable gate just before 7:00 and encountered a rather heavy-handed and dimwitted security guard whose job (for this week only) was to see that no evildoers had access to the Preakness horses.

He had a clipboard, and he had been instructed to register each visitor's name and record the purpose of his visit to the barn area at Pimlico.

John led off, told his name, spelled it several times, and informed the fellow that all of them had been invited to the barn of LeRoy Jolley. The guard painstakingly registered this information, dropping his pencil several times and making a few erasures in the process. The clock was now right on 7:00.

Next Terence Collier's name was slowly recorded, but without any significant hitches.

The third man was an Irishman named Peter Mulvagh. His brogue and unusual last name had the guard moving at a snail's pace. After several false starts, with laborious explanations about why this high level of security was essential, the guard registered Mr. Mulvagh.

But now the acid test was coming. The fourth gentleman was a Frenchman.

His name was Jean Baptiste De Gaste.

At this point John Finney could see that the opportunity to view Foolish Pleasure's work was slipping away.

The guard leaned his head in the car and asked, "Now what is your name, sir?"

John floorboarded it, as he yelled out, "*Tom Smith*, goddamn it!"

11

Some of the Straws That Stir the Drink

As fantastic and all-important as the horses have been in this man's sporting life — the colorful two-legged characters are the "straws that stir this intoxicating drink." Racing has hooked me up with many zany, wonderful, and unforgettable people. Directly and indirectly.

The group mentioned in this chapter is, to understate it, a diverse one. But they are all similar in that each of these characters conjures up warm and delectable memories.

Mickey Rooney

Sir Laurence Olivier stated that Mickey Rooney was the single best actor ever produced in America. I don't know about that, but in the late thirties and early forties he was the biggest box office attraction in the world. He had an affair with Lana Turner and married Ava Gardner. Those are noteworthy accomplishments.

I did, and do, think he's wonderful. Some years ago I wanted to name a horse for him. A mutual friend told Mickey of my wish and pleaded my case. And he was delighted. Mickey and I talked, and he gave me written permission for the name "Mickey Rooney" to be registered for a handsome bay colt by Nashua. Mickey and I got to be friends, and he bought a share in that colt.

Mickey Rooney, star of *National Velvet, The Black Stallion,* and other racing pictures, is no dummy about racehorses. Mickey has spent a lot of time at racetracks, was a stockholder in Santa Anita, and had owned horses before his Dogwood ventures. He told me he had once worked Seabiscuit five-eighths of a mile. I wonder about that because I think "Silent" Tom Smith, trainer of that great horse, was exceedingly picky about who did what with Seabiscuit. And it is pretty well established that Mickey's imagination has been known to run afoul of the facts.

At the time of Mickey's equine adventures with us, he was appearing in the wonderful burlesque review *Sugar Babies.* While our friendship and business relationship existed primarily on the phone, his equine involvements quickly expanded, and within a few months he owned shares in five horses.

Mickey did not sweat the small stuff, and the small stuff often included funding his purchases. He would say, "I'll take a share of that Vaguely Noble colt, and let me get a piece of that Nijinsky filly. Just tell Otis (his business manager) to take care of it!"

The problem was *he* did not tell Otis to take care of it! Otis knew nothing about it and did not wish to hear about it. He had heard about enough already. Consequently, it was tough to get paid for the horses Mickey "bought." Some of them almost died of old age before Mickey and his business manager got on the same page. This, of course, presented me with some fierce fiscal challenges, and finally Dogwood and Mickey got a divorce (not the first for either!).

At the outset of our relationship, Mickey, an avid gambler, instructed me to "bet five hundred every time a Dogwood horse runs." I knew this was not a good idea and told him, "Mickey, if my own dear, departed mother gave me such instructions, I would decline to follow them. I love you dearly, but I can't bet for you." Smartest move I ever made.

In those days and now, I went to New York fairly often and would always make arrangements to stop by the Broadhurst Theater and call on Mickey. I wanted to bring him up to date on his horses and, hopefully, discuss his always alarmingly delinquent account.

Business sessions with Mickey were experiences you would never forget.

The only time he could see you was just prior to his going on in *Sugar Babies*. Curtain was at eight. So Mickey would say "Meet me in my dressing room at 7:45." This impressed me as rather tight scheduling, so I would invariably arrive at 7:30. Mickey would invariably arrive at 7:55. The system suited me fine because when the meeting was over I would hustle into the theater and see the delightful show for the umpteenth time, having bought a ticket, you may be sure.

His dressing room was a ramshackle, disreputable hovel. Mickey had his favorite chair, in which he would hold court (for the brief time you got to see him). It was a huge, overstuffed chair that looked as if it might have been bought secondhand from the immigrants' lounge on Ellis Island. Much of the original cotton that held it together was now strewn around Mickey's dressing room.

Just before eight, Mickey would breeze in, strip down to his Jockey underwear, and plop into his chair. He would quickly run through the opening pleasantries and then recite a litany of projects he was going to undertake, most of which were creative, promising, and fascinating. If you ever complimented him or asked him about some accomplishment in the past, he would quickly brush you off and move into the future. (ME: "Mickey, your performance in *Bill* was absolutely incredible. You've got to win an Emmy for that!" ROONEY: "Yeah, but lemme tell you — Martha Raye and I are going to do a musical based on the comic strip *Maggie and Jiggs*!")

Now it would be 8:05. I could hear the overture strike up. As it finished, Mickey would be enthusing over another project. I could hear audience laughter and applause as Ann Miller, his co-star, finished her first number. With one nude leg thrown over the arm of the battle-worn chair, Mickey would be explaining his ten rules for a happy life. I would offer, "Now, Mickey, I know I'm taking too much of your time, but let me ask you about that last filly you bought a piece of..."

"Aw, don't worry. Did you hear about the commercial I'm doing for the Animal's Rights Foundation...they're going to..."

My watch read 8:20. The musical has now been going on for twenty minutes, and the star is still in his underwear! A barely audible knocking signal comes at the door. Still Mickey is talking, now discoursing on his religious conversion. I can hear two comics on stage, and their routine is bringing down the house. Still he talks; I listen.

Suddenly, as if an electric impulse has surged through his short, fat body, he is out of the chair. He grabs a clown suit off the coat rack, leaps into it, zips up the front, grabs my hand, pumps it once, and goes flying out the door. As I walk down the rickety stairs, I can hear him on stage, belting out lyrics.

"If you knew Suzy like I know Suzy. Oh what a girl...!"

Ah, Mickey Rooney.

I wish I had him back.

John D. Marsh

"Curmudgeon" should be defined in *Webster's Dictionary* with simply a photograph of John D. Marsh. The likeness would portray a very Prussian-like, smallish man with a crew cut on a balding head. Thick, horn-rimmed glasses would enhance a rather owlish, stern, but otherwise essentially poker-faced expression. Add the bristling white mustache of a cavalry officer, then stick a big, fat cigar right in the dead center of his mouth. John D. Marsh.

He was a good guy, but a tough, minor-league curmudgeon, and he scared the living hell out of a lot of people.

A prominent Virginia breeder, John campaigned a big stable of horses, all homebreds, on three Eastern seaboard fronts. He was heavily involved with the Virginia Thoroughbred Breeders Association, the Breeders' Cup, and the Thoroughbred Owners and Breeders Association (TOBA).

When he returned from the U.S. Army Air Force at the end of World War II, he founded the Washington, D.C.-based Variable Annuity Life Insurance Company, creating a product of life insurance and annuities backed by common stocks. And with that, the author has depleted his knowledge of that subject, for which you will be glad. Marsh made a lot of money and got into racehorses — that's the main point.

He attacked racing with the same motto employed in every phase of his life and career: precision!

I first met him when he recruited me as a trustee for TOBA.

When I went to my first meeting, I could quickly tell that John was a man after my own heart. He was most impatient, did not suffer fools gladly (if at all!), and in meetings was not a stickler for parliamentary procedure, dismissing the existence of Robert's Rules of Order.

At the time, the president of TOBA was a very sweet lady, quite capable, but somewhat tentative in running a meeting and completely disinclined to "crack the whip." She had a soft, halting voice that bespoke her reticent nature.

John, not one of the pioneers of the feminist movement, almost caused this leader a nervous breakdown. John was a tad hard of hearing, and when this lady's voice began to falter while on some troublesome point, John would yell out, "Speak up, goddamn it!"

When a motion on the floor was being thoroughly scrutinized (too thoroughly, in John's opinion), he would help move it along by screaming, "Call for the question, goddamn it." That usually expedited the vote.

John Marsh loved the races. He campaigned three divisions in the summer. He had a string in New York, another at Laurel, and the lesser lights were at Penn National.

But he particularly loved Saratoga and spent much of the meeting there with Hilda, his fine and steadfast wife of many years. She brought dedication and efficiency to John's way of carrying out certain operational procedures, especially those of a social nature.

Each August the couple would "entertain" with a cocktail party at the Saratoga Golf and Polo Club. R.S.V.P. invitations were sent out several weeks in advance, and incoming responses were recorded with precision.

At the party John Marsh stood at the front door of the club with a huge clipboard cradled in his arm. When you arrived, John put a big checkmark by your name. This was accompanied by a curt nod of approval, and then John waved you through. If you had not responded but showed up, this necessitated a lengthy interrogation about your lack of communication, your name was marked accordingly, you were, of course, chastised for your sloppiness, and then you were allowed to participate in the "festivities."

If you had indicated that you would attend but did not make an appearance…then your ass was mud forevermore!

John was not so much concerned with generating cheery social intercourse as he was in squaring up the tally on the clipboard. First things first.

Frank Alexander, who has trained for Dogwood for close to twenty-five years, had horses for John when our association first began. Like almost everyone who knew John Marsh, Frank liked him immensely but recognized that you had to conform to Marsh's program if you were on Marsh's team. In Frank's case, he had to fill out a six-page questionnaire before he was hired.

In the late seventies Joe Cantey had the New York horses, Frank had the Maryland division, and some other guy had the cheapies at Penn National. A monthly meeting was held on the farm the first Monday night and Tuesday of each month. Attendance was mandatory.

The trainers would arrive in late afternoon and be assigned to their lodging. They would then convene at the main house for a brief cocktail hour. At six on the dot, Mrs. Marsh would activate the music system and appropriate classical music would begin. At that very moment the trainers, key farm personnel, John, and maybe Mrs. Marsh would sit down for dinner. After dinner the men would repair to the den where films of great races of the past would be shown (Mr. Cantey having been entrusted to bring these from the New York Racing Association library). This would be followed by a seminar of training procedures conducted by the three conditioners present.

At a sensible hour this would be terminated and all hands would retire, so that the next day's wake-up time of 6 a.m. would not be jeopardized. The first time Frank attended, he was, of course, slightly green on procedural matters. John Marsh told his wife to get Frank an alarm clock. Frank, being helpful, protested, "Mr. Marsh, I don't need any alarm clock. I've been getting up earlier than that all my life."

"Get him an alarm clock!" John repeated.

The next morning at six, alarms rang all over the house, followed by a rousing set of John Phillip Sousa march music piped in on the intercom system. "Breakfast is on the table," came the announcement at the conclusion of *The Washington Post March.*

After breakfast it was off to the training barn to watch the stock train. Another meeting, including all key personnel on the farm, followed. John Marsh would make his own observations on the way things were going and would deal with special gusto on "the damned outrageous vet bills. Sound horses don't need all that damned medication!"

Each trainer would then report on every horse in his care, and there would be tactful critiques between racetrack and farm people. This was followed by a farewell lunch.

The guests would be served a sensible, nutritious lunch. John Marsh would have only a diet root beer, accompanied by a silver plate on which were arrayed the pills he required daily.

Once, Frank Alexander, in an audacious moment of good-natured impudence, reached over and removed the silver plate housing the Marsh pill allotment.

"Here, now! What the hell are you doing with my pills?" barked John Marsh.

"Well, Mr. Marsh, if those horses don't need all that medication, neither should the boss-man," Frank explained.

A deathly silence enveloped the luncheon. Guests looked apprehensively at the host, waiting for the explosion. John Marsh stared at Frank for a moment. Then he grinned appreciatively. "Oh hell, go on and eat your damned lunch!"

Lester and the Pheasant

Since the dawn of Thoroughbred racing, no human being has spawned as many stories as has English jockey Lester Piggott.

One reason for his notoriety has to do with many, here and abroad, thinking him to be the greatest rider who ever lived.

Another is his personality. It is fashioned not from traits of exuberance or clownish behavior; nor from charm, warmth, or jovial wit; and God forbid that the milk of human kindness would have contributed to Lester's persona!

The makeup of Lester Piggott would have more to do with his fanatical determination to win; his ruthless approach to securing the right horses to do it with; his taciturn, dour, penurious nature; and his completely independent, mischievous, impertinent demeanor.

These are not usually endearing character traits. Therefore, you would think Lester Piggott would surely be the most detested man in European racing. Not so. While not beloved perhaps, he is accepted and sought after socially. Why? Probably because he is authentic. During his years as a jockey, Piggott could, and did, deliver the goods better than anyone else ever had. He was the king.

The following simple incident probably demonstrates clearly all of the foregoing observations on the intricacies of Lester Piggott.

Lester was recently invited to go pheasant shooting by Harry Carr, a prominent English horseman, on his property at Wickhambrook, near Newmarket.

Lester was standing in a line of guns between two well-known jockeys of yesteryear, Jimmy Lindley and Joe Mercer. Quite a few birds had come Lester's way, and none thus far had suffered any ill effects.

Toward the end of the drive when the beaters and their dogs had approached to within fifty to sixty yards, a large cock pheasant came running down the fence line.

To Carr's absolute horror, Piggott quickly threw his shotgun to his shoulder and took aim.

Harry shouted, "No, no, Lester! You cannot shoot it when it is running!"

"The bugger won't stand still!" Lester replied and quickly followed this with a blast that practically blew the bird in half.

Sam Huff

In 1960 CBS televised a one-hour primetime special devoted to portraying the ferocious nature of one of the greatest football players who ever lived.

Its title was *The Violent World of Sam Huff.*

Sam Huff was at that time, from 1956 to 1963, linebacker for the New York Giants, and he brought a new meaning to mayhem on the football field.

Today, no longer dedicated to ferocity, Sam is a major player in the world of Thoroughbred horse racing. With his partner, Carol Holden, he both breeds and races horses. Sam is conscientiously active, and most vocal, in various organizations seeking the betterment of our sport and industry. He has a job as a vice president of the Marriott Corporation and also does radio color commentary on the Washington Redskins football games. His career is associated chiefly with the New York Giants, but his playing days ended in 1967, with the Redskins.

He and Carol have a weekly radio show on racing, emanating from their home in Middleburg, Virginia. A native West Virginian, Sam Huff in 1987 created and promoted a day of racing in which Charles Town Race Track would offer hundreds of thousands of dollars in five races exclusively for West Virginia-breds. This was called the West Virginia Breeders Classics. It was odds-on not to get off the ground, but Sam approached the task like he approached Jimmy Brown coming at him off-tackle. He meant to prevail. In 2002, Classics will have its fifteenth renewal, and ESPN will cover it.

Sam Huff says the three most difficult, complicated fields of endeavor are politics, horse racing, and football. "And I'm involved in all three!" he laments.

But he adores horse racing, and his fervor was bolstered a few years back when he bred a wonderful race filly. Typical of our game, this mating came about not by a brilliant understanding of the gene pool nor the skillful practice of animal husbandry, but through a nutty fluke resulting from a speech he couldn't get out of making.

The Boy Scouts were having a statewide meeting in

February in Parkersburg, West Virginia, and his friend Smoot Fahlgren, a prominent businessman and horse owner, asked Sam to bring to these young men an inspirational message. The topic was striving, sticking to it, never giving up, and...well, you get the idea.

Speech day came, and one of the worst blizzards in its history visited West Virginia. On top of that, Sam had the flu. With a three-hour mountainous drive facing him, he called and said he simply did not see how he could get there. Smoot refused to let a little snow and flu stop the unstoppable Sam. He lectured him vigorously on the theme of the advertised speech.

Sam begrudgingly went, made an inspired talk, and later received an unexpected honorarium in the form of a stallion season to an unheralded new sire named Alwasmi.

Huff's mare Burst of Sound was bred on this season. The result was Bursting Forth, one of the finest distance runners of her generation. When she won the prestigious Bewitch Stakes at Keeneland, so delighted was the old linebacker that he vaulted over the grandstand fence in his frenzy to get to the infield winner's circle on that congested day at Keeneland.

He has since maintained that that win was a greater thrill than any championship football game he ever played.

Professionals in any sport or occupation deal with success and adversity in a routine manner almost every day. Most develop an understated, matter-of-fact, and seemingly callous way of communicating.

Doctors don't emerge from the operating room "high-fiving" one another, nor sobbing and gnashing their teeth, depending on the outcome of an operation. But they feel the significance of the situation deeply, and they try as hard as they can.

So it is with horse people. When a good horse goes wrong, it is devastating. But "what ifs" and post mortems are not productive. So the pros tend to be verbally quite economical in dealing with their anguish. This does not mean they are callous.

Sam tells this inside version of a famous incident. It had a happy ending, but it demonstrated the rough brusqueness of football players in their locker room jargon.

In 1960 the New York Giants were playing their bitter rivals, the Philadelphia Eagles, in New York's Yankee Stadium. It was early in the season, and baseball had been played there in recent weeks. Therefore, portions of where the diamond had been were bare and hard as rock.

Early in the second quarter, Frank Gifford, the great Giants halfback, took a pass from Charley Connerly on the dead run just at the very point where home plate had been. Just as he gathered in the ball, Chuck Bednarik, the vicious Eagles linebacker, was driving full-tilt into him. He creamed him. Gifford's helmet flew off as he was slammed brutally into the rock-hard clay. The ball was fumbled understandably, and the Eagles recovered.

Gifford was out like a light. His close friend, Sam Huff, recognized a serious injury, and as he came on the field with the defensive team, he had mixed feelings.

"First, I was worried about Frank. He was hurt bad. Second though, as a linebacker I *had* to admire Bednarik's tackle! What a beauty! Picture perfect! Textbook! I loved the tackle...would have given anything to have been on the delivery end of a hit like that," he said.

Sam trotted past the still motionless form of Gifford, who was white as a sheet. The team doctor and trainers were hovering over him, preparing to lift him on a stretcher and rush him to the clinic.

Sam shook his head, turned and said to his teammate, the defensive tackle Dick Modzelewski, "Mo, that sumbitch is dead!"

Mo nodded solemnly, "Yeah, Sam."

Gifford, on a gurney now, was rushed off the field for emergency medical attention. The game commenced, and the first half was played out.

The hospital clinic at Yankee Stadium was adjacent to the Giants' dressing room; in fact, you had to go through it to get to the clinic.

The Giants came back into their dressing room and were sprawled on benches in front of their lockers, catching their breaths before getting reorganized for the second half.

As Sam, Mo, and the Giants were resting, heads between their knees, the door of the clinic opened and out came a gurney being pushed by two attendants. On it was the form of a human being completely covered by a sheet.

Sam spotted it and his heart sank. He grabbed at Mo's arm, pointed, and wailed, "Mo, I told you that sumbitch was dead!"

Minutes later came word that Frank Gifford was in stable condition but had a severe concussion.

The sumbitch was not dead.

The corpse was that of a poor security guard who had died of a heart attack.

I first met Sam through a close mutual friend, Furman Bisher, longtime sports editor of *The Atlanta Journal and Constitution*, with whom Sam owned some racehorses. Despite his football reputation for aggression, off the gridiron Sam Huff has always been a warm, pleasant fellow and as good a friend as you could find.

If you saw him in a restaurant, you would not conclude: "Ohmigosh, that man has got to be a professional football player!" He just looks like a good-sized, handsome fellow much younger than his years. If you were a bully and looking for a fight, you would certainly not want to target Sam…but neither would he be picked out of a crowd as one whose violent ways inspired an hour-long television special.

I named a big, strapping Unbridled colt "Sam Huff." I am afraid he did not come close to inspiring any TV coverage.

Tex Sutton

A horseman's horseman was a seamy-faced Texan named Halford Ewel Sutton, known by everyone as Tex.

This old boy had done it all. On the racetrack Tex had walked hots and been a groom, exercise rider, and "valet to the stars." In the jocks' room, he took care of Eddie Arcaro, Johnny Adams, and Bill Boland.

In the early fifties, while assisting prominent horseman Ralph Lowe in buying and culling stock for his racing stable, Tex stumbled into what at the time was a badly needed occupation. He became a shipping agent for horses, and his pioneered specialty was air travel. At one point he represented as many as ninety-two different horsemen. He got to where he was by buying and selling horses at sales on their behalf and was flying horses all over the world.

Tex Sutton had the face of a cowboy. If he hadn't been so skinny, he could have been a "Marlboro Man." His countenance was a map that told the story of his life, and it looked like forty miles of bad Texas roads. Woodie Guthrie used to sing a ballad called "Hard Travlin." Tex Sutton could have inspired the lyrics.

Tex was universally liked and respected. He led a demanding life in that he spent much of it in the cargo hold of a plane or on loading ramps, wrestling with one thousand pounds of romping, stomping meat.

So when Tex got to a destination — and only then — he liked to relax and have a drink. By no means was Tex an alcoholic, but he could be classified as a dedicated drinker. Because of this tendency, and exacerbated by the fact that he had an ailment known as diffuse Lewy Body disease, Tex often shook like a leaf.

There used to be a woman around Lexington who was sort of a quasi-bloodstock agent, public relations specialist, and a very chatty gadfly in general.

She knew Tex, as everyone in the horse business did, and she encountered him one day in the track kitchen. He was having a cup of coffee, and he clearly had a severe case of the shakes.

Not known for her diplomacy, this gal decided she would just get to the bottom of Tex's tremors.

"Now, Tex, let me ask you something," she started in. "I've been wondering why you shake so much. You just shake all the time. Now why is that? Shake, shake, shake! Tell me — why do you shake so much?"

With the steely-eyed glint of a man who wouldn't brook an excessive amount of familiarity, Tex stared at her incredulously for a few moments.

Then he moved a little closer to her, cocked his head, squinted hard at her, and said, "I'm just shaking with pride! Cause I mind my own goddamned business!"

Airborne Wellborne

The title of the book is *Rascals and Racehorses — A Sporting Man's Life*. Well, this is about two rascals. Or, to be charitable to the author, a rascal and a sporting man. The event was inspired by an inexplicable obsession that came over me while racing horses at Saratoga in the late summer of 1993.

I decided that it behooved me to jump out of an airplane — with a parachute, of course.

I have no earthly idea what triggered this. I am not an enthusiastic flyer and do not care for heights. Perhaps I saw a last opportunity to wave good-bye to my youth, unmistakably disappearing. This may have been a final salute to the tumultuous, zany, risk-laden springtime of my life. Who knows?

When I got back to Aiken, this desire was stronger than ever, and I researched the possibilities of such an undertaking. I found that the airport in Walterboro, South Carolina, offered skydiving. I called the Walterboro Airport and had a conversation with a man identified as a "jump master."

I asked him about procedural matters: clothing, shoes, insurance, training time required, and lastly, whether it mattered if I were sixty-six years of age. "Doesn't matter to me," he helpfully answered.

I was surprised to learn that a couple of hours of training would suffice. So we agreed that I would drive to Walterboro on the following Tuesday, "train" from ten to noon, and then make my jump that afternoon.

"To whom am I speaking?" I asked, as the arrangements were finalized.

"Airborne Wellborne," was the proud reply.

I had told Anne of this idea while in Saratoga and later reiterated my interest when we got back to Aiken. At that point she said rather absentmindedly, "Oh, that might be fun." Now I told her of my specific appointment with Airborne Wellborne, and she became considerably more tuned-in to the project. She was not against it exactly, but she was quite able to control any display of enthusiasm she might have felt.

I checked with my insurance man, who did say that insurance would cover any mishap (a euphemism, if there ever were one), but if I planned to embrace this sport as an ongoing hobby, we might have to rethink my coverage.

The appointed day in September arrived, and I motored by myself to Walterboro, an hour and a half away. I must admit at this point my zeal to jump was not strong. But I had said to others, and myself, that I was going to do it, and now I simply had to jump.

It was hot as hell, and when I arrived at the facility, it did not impress me a great deal. There were several dilapidated

Quonset huts, some rather greasy-looking small airplanes, and a few uninspired human beings slouching around.

No one seemed to know why Airborne was not on hand for our training session.

I had imagined a much more spit-and-polish operation. Where were the smartly uniformed jumping instructors, the eagle-eyed mechanics peering worriedly into engines, the earnest young men painstakingly packing parachutes under the watchful eye of a supervisor? Where was the lunchroom or at least the snack bar? Not at the Walterboro Airport. Nor was Airborne Wellborne.

About 10:30 a.m. I was standing dispiritedly by my auto in the dusty parking lot. I had gotten to this point; this was the day I was going to do my number; and I hated like hell to abort the project.

Suddenly I heard a motor, looked up, and saw a cloud of dust a quarter mile down the sandy airport approach road. A motorcycle was nearing. The bike screeched into the parking lot and skidded to a halt near me. The passenger was a strange-looking man. He was attired in cut-off jeans, heavily fringed. He had no shirt or head covering, and he had a tonsorial treatment that looked as if Harpo Marx had inspired it.

He looked at me, shook his head groggily, and said, "I'm Airborne Wellborne. Man, I been ridin' this damned thing all the way from Daytona…and I got a hellacious hangover! You ready?"

Pretty soon we got right down to business. Airborne schooled me in various procedures, not all of which were entirely comforting. Landing seemed to be the most hazardous. He told me that if I landed in a lake, I should be sure to avoid coming up under the chute. "Swim out until you're sure its not still spread out above you. Otherwise, you'll get tangled up in the chute and you'll drown, sure as hell!" Airborne helpfully explained.

Other perils included landing in trees and power lines.

My jumpmaster advised, "Now, if you land in a tree, you want to be sure to protect your groin." I was quite sure that would have been my natural inclination. "But if you land on a power line…well, there ain't anything you can do." His voice trailed off hopelessly.

"When you drop, arch your back and count slowly to four. If your static line chute has not opened by then, you had better be reaching for your auxiliary parachute," he told me. "But I've got to tell you, you don't just jump out of the airplane. When I give you the signal you have got to go hand over hand out onto the struts (the supports going diagonally from the fuselage to the wings on this Piper Cub). If you don't work your way out to about six feet, you'll hit the tail when you drop."

This was not good news. I had envisioned screaming "Geronimo" and then leaping boldly into the wild blue. "Hitting the silk," I thought we called it.

We practiced "going out on the struts." I did not care for the idea, but I could do it. At this point, I could do anything if we would just get started.

Airborne looked thoughtfully at me and said, "Well, I guess that's all we can do. I suppose you're ready to jump."

I leapt to my feet.

Airborne consulted his watch. It was about 1:15. "But first, I've got to go pick up my little girl at school. She gets out at two o'clock. I'll try to be back here by 2:30, and maybe we'll take a crack at it."

Airborne was nothing if not professional!

The Walterboro Flying Service did not offer food or any refreshments, nor was there an air-cooled lounge for us who were about to skydive, nor had I brought anything to read. I was reluctant to leave the premises for fear that Mr. Wellborne might return early and be willing to accelerate the schedule. So I sat under a tree in temperatures that hovered near the hundred-degree mark and meditated about the wonderful experience in which I was participating. I thought about calling home but figured there should be only one call — upon completion of the mission.

After what seemed an eternity I heard the sound of Airborne's motorcycle, and he wheeled into the parking lot.

"You ready, you think?" he asked.

"You bet!" I told him.

We found the pilot, who seemed slightly annoyed he would be expected to fly on such a hot day. But he cranked up the Piper Cub while the jump master and student went over the checklist, and I was fitted with my chutes — static line and auxiliary.

The airplane taxied out into the sunshine. Alarmingly, it was practically jet-black with grease that had leaked from its single engine through long years of use. I observed no door on the passenger side. This disturbed me until I found out that the door was removed to facilitate my departure out onto the struts. We got aboard — the jump master in the back and the eager student sitting on the floor (there was also no seat for the same reason).

We chugged out to the end of the runway, turned into the wind, and awaited clearance to take off.

Then I remembered something. I had been told to bring a camera. While dangling from the struts, awaiting Airborne's high-sign signal to drop, I could have been photographed by the pilot. I did bring the camera but forgot to put it on the plane. It was in the hangar. Should I advise the two men that we must taxi back so that I could retrieve my camera?

No.

So we took off and climbed our way up to 4,500 feet, with me looking anxiously back at Airborne from time to time. He was sleepily picking his teeth.

But soon Airborne hooked me up and reminded me again to go at least six feet out on the struts to avoid being mangled by the tail. Then he suddenly became very military, barking out, "Take your position!"

With that, I turned sideways, put my feet on the step right under where the door was supposed to be, and gazed down at the tiny pastures and cornfields below, with at least a fleeting thought about lakes, trees, and power lines.

"Out on the struts," came the brisk command (damned welcome, at this point).

Out I went, hand over hand, hanging on for dear life, with my legs outstretched behind me, as the plane wheezed along at eighty-five miles per hour. When the magic six feet had been reached, I looked back hopefully at good old Airborne. He looked at me for what seemed to be an eternity, then, in a gesture befitting the Screaming Eagles of the 101st Airborne, he clenched his fist, extended his thumb upward, and jerked it dramatically.

I dropped. Oh my God, did I ever drop! I never felt such force. I screamed out the count, "One thousand, two thousand...." I could not hear myself, but it didn't matter. About the time I mouthed "three," I did hear — and felt — a huge "whoomp!" The chute had opened, and what a lovely sight it was.

Now I was floating slowly downward amidst a wonderful absence of any sound. This was delightful and a moment almost worth all the anguish. What a shockingly peaceful experience!

I had forgotten that I was fitted with a two-way radio to expedite my journey to the ground, and suddenly the silence was interrupted with a ghostly voice: "You're doing fine, Mr. Campbell!" This was some unknown team member on the ground.

About thirty seconds later, as I was drifting earthward, the voice said, "That's fine. Now turn left a bit." To accomplish this, you were to tug on your left shroud line. "That's it. Turn left. Turn left. Turn *right.*" I followed instructions.

Suddenly, "No, no, not right. I mean left!" I turned left. But now, I had gotten off course for the desired landing on the soft grass adjacent to the runway, and I was headed for very hard concrete on the runway itself. I suppose he could have talked me into a correction that would have improved my approach and made for a more comfortable conclusion, but he must have felt that he should leave well enough alone. There was only silence.

About ten feet above the runway, I pulled heavily on both shroud lines to make my landing more gradual and ease my way onto the ground. My heels hit the runway, slid out from under me, and I put out my forearm to break my fall. It absorbed most of the contact with the concrete. In a second I was sitting on the runway. I was down, but with a badly skinned forearm. But I *was* down — safely and successfully.

Soon the grimy aircraft and Airborne landed. He came over to me as I walked back to the hangar with my parachute gathered up in my arms. At that point I thought again about the camera. I got it and asked Airborne to take a photo of me standing by the hangar with my chute billowing in front of me. It was not very dramatic, but it was better than nothing.

With an official flourish, Airborne signed my "logbook," with various notations about the weak and strong points exhibited in my first jump.

There was space for additional jumps. I still have the logbook.

The spaces are still blank.

* * *

There are blank pages also in my "future book" of horse racing. But these I do look forward to filling up. With eagerness and optimism.

I have expended my repertoire of repeatable anecdotes, but the arena in which we toil and play is a bountiful source of plenty more. If you keep showing up, you will hear them.

I am no "spring chicken" (although rarely am I aware of it!). Therefore, it is natural that I am asked occasionally — usually with some degree of tact — about retirement from the pursuit of fast horses.

I realize how lucky I am when the answer is unhesitatingly: "Not until I drop!"

What a great life.

Acknowledgments

Anne Dodd Campbell

On December 16, 1958, I walked up to the sign-out desk at Main Hall at Agnes Scott College in Decatur, Georgia, and rather sheepishly asked for Anne Dodd. Sheepish I was because I doubted that it was appropriate for me to be trekking to a church-affiliated women's college in a borrowed automobile to have a blind date with a person about a decade younger than me. Despite glowing promotion from a credible "matchmaker," my heart was not completely in it.

At age thirty-one I was an impecunious advertising copywriter, barely a year along on the rocky road to revamping what seemed to be an irreparably bad reputation.

I waited uncomfortably. I was clad in rather conventional business attire: coat and tie, Harris Tweed overcoat, and a snap-brim fedora. Surrounded by Georgia Tech and Emory collegians in sweaters and windbreakers, I stood out like a sore thumb. I thought, What the hell am I doing here?

Then the young lady came in, waved gaily toward me (clearly the one who easily fit the description she'd been given), and proceeded to sign out for the evening. When she came over to greet me, I quickly arrived at two conclusions: terrific smile, outstanding figure.

I felt better.

In the next few months I discovered a thousand additional attributes.

We married that summer, even though Anne and her family had received dire warnings about my well-established wildness. These warnings were well founded I must admit. But they were disregarded, and, as it turned out, they should have been.

No couple ever went on to have a more exciting, colorful, interesting, and ideal life.

She married me when I was poor as a church mouse, owed a lot of money, but was beginning to see a smidgen of daylight. If it was tough, she did not know it. And it got pretty good pretty soon. She was always "in my corner."

Not once has this woman ever doubted the successful outcome of any venture I have proposed. In fact, she led the cheering, then did everything in her power to put it over the top.

It behooves me to end this book with this salute to Anne Campbell, the most wonderful wife in history. To me.

With all my heart I thank her — the ideal companion on a stupendous journey.

Photo Credits

Man o' War and Will Harbut . . . . (James W. Sames III)
Phoenix Hotel . . . . . (Ron Garrison/*Lexington Herald-Leader*)
Black Gold . . . . (*The Blood-Horse*)
Rosa Hoots. . . . . (H.C. Ashby)
John Gaver. . . . . (Dell Hancock)
Aiken Trials . . . . (courtesy of Shoney's Aiken)
Clayton O'Quinn . . . . (*The Florida Horse*)
A young Cot Campbell. . . . . (courtesy of the author)
Shoestring Stable . . . . (courtesy of the author)
Sheikh Bin Had . . . . (courtesy of the author)
Jan Verzal . . . . (courtesy of the author)
Neiman sketch . . . . (courtesy of the author)
Olympia-Stella Moore match race . . . . (Tropical Park)
Cinzano . . . . (Peter Chew)
Kelso and dogs . . . . (courtesy of the author)
Greyhound . . . . (*The Horseman and Fair World*)
Birmingham Turf Club . . . . (Louise E. Reinagel)
Angel Penna . . . . (Louise E. Reinagel)
The Jones Boys and Citation . . . . (Churchill Downs)
Buddy Raines . . . . (Barbara D. Livingston)
Bob Smith . . . . (Bert Clark Thayer)
Leslie Combs II . . . . (Milt Toby)
Warner L. Jones, Will Farish, and Cot Campbell
. . . . (courtesy of the author)
John Finney . . . . (*The Blood-Horse*)
Mickey Rooney . . . . (Shigeki Kikkawa)
Lester Piggott . . . . (John Crofts Photography)
Sam Huff . . . . (Anne M. Eberhardt)
Cot Campbell, skydiver . . . . (courtesy of the author)
Anne and Cot Campbell . . . . (Jan Perret)

About the Author

W. Cothran Campbell is a pioneer of Thoroughbred racehorse partnerships, founding Dogwood Stable in 1969 for that purpose. Since the stable's inception, Campbell has introduced more than 1,200 people to racing, and Dogwood has purchased more than $100 million worth of bloodstock.

Dogwood Stable clients include numerous current and former chairmen or presidents of Fortune 500 corporations and stars from the entertainment and sports industries. Among North America's most successful racing stables, Dogwood has campaigned such top horses as Preakness Stakes winner Summer Squall, two-year-old filly champion Storm Song, and steeplechase champion Inlander.

Campbell formerly served as chairman of Burton-Campbell, Inc., one of the South's largest advertising agencies, before taking up the reins of Dogwood Stable full time. He has served on numerous Thoroughbred industry boards and is a trustee of the Thoroughbred Owners and Breeders Association and board member of the National Museum of Racing and Hall of Fame. In addition, he is a founding member of the National Thoroughbred Association and a co-founder of the Georgia Thoroughbred Breeders Association. In 1992 Campbell received the John W. Galbreath Award for entrepreneurial excellence and leadership in the horse industry, presented by the University of Louisville.

Campbell's first book, *Lightning in a Jar — Catching Racing Fever,* was published in 2000.

He and his wife, Anne, live in Aiken, South Carolina. They have two daughters and five grandchildren.

Other Titles from Eclipse Press

At the Wire
Horse Racing's Greatest Moments

Baffert
Dirt Road to the Derby

The Calumet Collection
A History of the Calumet Trophies

Cigar
America's Horse (revised edition)

Country Life Diary
(revised edition)

Crown Jewels of Thoroughbred Racing

Dynasties
Great Thoroughbred Stallions

Etched in Stone

Four Seasons of Racing

Great Horse Racing Mysteries

Hoofprints in the Sand
Wild Horses of the Atlantic Coast

Horse Racing's Holy Grail
The Epic Quest for the Kentucky Derby

Investing in Thoroughbreds
Strategies for Success

Lightning in a Jar
Catching Racing Fever

Matriarchs
Great Mares of the 20th Century

Olympic Equestrian

Ride of Their Lives
The Triumphs and Turmoil of Today's Top Jockeys

Royal Blood

Thoroughbred Champions
Top 100 Racehorses of the 20th Century

Women in Racing
In Their Own Words

Thoroughbred Legends® Series

Affirmed and Alydar
Citation
Dr. Fager
Forego
Go for Wand
John Henry
Man o' War
Nashua
Native Dancer
Personal Ensign
Round Table
Ruffian
Seattle Slew
Spectacular Bid
Sunday Silence
Swaps
War Admiral

A Division of The Blood-Horse, Inc.
Publishers Since 1916

RASCALS
&
RACEHORSES
Mickey Rooney
Seabiscuit
Sheikh Bin Had
Fred Hooper
Al Capone
Kelso
Warner Jones
Leslie Combs
Jimmy Jones
Eddie Arcaro